A
Devotional
Treasury
from the
Early Church

compiled by
GEORGIA HARKNESS

A
Devotional
Treasury
from the
Early Church

ABINGDON PRESS
Nashville & New York

A DEVOTIONAL TREASURY FROM THE EARLY CHURCH

Copyright © 1968 by Abingdon Press

Library of Congress Catalog Card Number: 68-17436

Scripture quotations unless otherwise noted are from the
Revised Standard Version of the Bible, copyrighted 1946
and 1952 by the Division of Christian Education, National
Council of Churches, and are used by permission.

Quotations from *The Apostolic Fathers*, Vols. I, II, translated by Krisopp Lake, copyright 1912/13 G. P. Putnam's Sons, are used by permission of Putnam's & Coward-
McCann.
Quotations from *The Apostolic Fathers: An American
Translation* by Edgar J. Goodspeed, copyright 1950 Harper & Brothers, are reprinted with the permission of Harper
& Row, Publishers, Inc., New York.
Quotations from *Early Christian Fathers*, LCC, Vol. I,
edited and translated by Cyril C. Richardson. Published
in the U.S.A. by The Westminster Press, 1953. Used by
permission.

SET UP, PRINTED, AND BOUND BY THE
PARTHENON PRESS, AT NASHVILLE,
TENNESSEE, UNITED STATES OF AMERICA

Acknowledgments

I wish gratefully to acknowledge my indebtedness to G. P. Putnam's Sons for permission to use translations by Kirsopp Lake in *The Apostolic Fathers*, Volumes I and II of the Loeb Classical Library; to Harper & Row for translations by Edgar J. Goodspeed in *The Apostolic Fathers: An American Translation;* and to the Westminster Press for translations by Cyril C. Richardson, Massey Hamilton Shepherd, Jr., and Eugene R. Fairweather in *Early Christian Fathers,* Volume I of the Library of Christian Classics. I have tried in each case to use the translation best suited to a particular excerpt, and this has resulted in a nearly equal distribution among these three sources. The location of each excerpt by chapter in the original document and also by page in the translation may be found in the references at the end of this compilation.

For the text of the Odes of Solomon I have used primarily the classic translation by Rendel Harris and Alphonse Mingana in *The Odes and Psalms of Solomon,* Volume II, published by Longmans, Green and Co. in 1920. In some instances, which have been indicated in the references, I have adopted the revisions of the Harris-Mingana version made by Michael MarYosip in his book *The Oldest Christian Hymn-Book,* published by Gresham's in 1948. I am much indebted to the John Rylands Library of Manchester, England, and Mrs. Mar-Yosip for permission to use these sources and thus to make available some moving poetry which will, I suspect, be new to most readers.

Contents

Introduction 11

First Clement 19

    1. Called and Sanctified by the Will of God 23
    2. God's Gifts of Peace in All Nature 25
    3. One Body in Christ 26
    4. In Praise of Love 28
    5. A Pastoral Prayer 30
    6. Blessing and Doxology 32

Ignatius 34

    1. Of Faith and Love 38
    2. Of Speech and Silence 40

3. There Is Nothing Better than Peace ... 41
4. One in Christ and the Bishop 42
5. One Altar, One Eucharist 44
6. One Faith 45
7. Jesus Christ the Word 46
8. Farewell in Jesus Christ 48

Polycarp 50

1. Let Us Hold Constantly to Our Hope .. 54
2. Build One Another Up 55
3. The Martyrdom of Polycarp 57

The Shepherd of Hermas 64

1. Living Stones 67
2. Strong Foundations 70
3. The Working of Ill Temper 72
4. To Live to God 74
5. The Sum of the Matter 75

The Letter of Barnabas 78

1. Let Knowledge Be Perfected Along with
   Faith 82
2. Counsel for Evil Days 83
3. Of True Fasting 85
4. Eat No Unclean Thing 87
5. A Temple of the Lord 88

The Didache 91

1. The Way of Life 94
2. The Way of Death 98

3. Two Eucharistic Prayers 99
4. For Peace and Purity 101

Second Clement 103

1. The New Being in Christ 106
2. Words and Works 107
3. Two Worlds 109
4. The Contest and the Crown 111
5. Wait in Hope and Single-Mindedness ..112
6. The Living Church 114

The Letter to Diognetus 117

1. How to Listen 120
2. The Church in the World 121
3. All Things Were Made Through Him ..124
4. The Imitation of God 126
5. The Eternal and Present Word 127
6. The Tree of Knowledge and the Tree
   of Life 128

The Odes of Solomon 131

1. The Crown of Life 135
2. A Hymn to the Love of God 136
3. Living Water for All to Drink 137
4. A Good Captivity for Freedom 139
5. Words and the Word 141
6. A Psalm of Praise and Petition 143
7. The Glory of the Lord and His Beauty ..144
8. A Priest of the Lord 146

9

9. Who Can Write the Songs of the Lord? . 148
10. The Lord Is My Hope 150
11. Water from the Living Fountain 151
12. Believe and Live 152
13. The Dew of the Lord 153
14. Hallelujah! 155

References 157

Introduction

The purpose of this book is to make available some excerpts from the rich treasure house of Christian devotion to be found in the writings which have been preserved to us from the earliest days of the Christian church. The selections begin where the Bible leaves off and extend approximately through the middle of the second century of our era.

Most seminary libraries possess impressive sets of quarto volumes containing the works of the ante-Nicene and post-Nicene fathers, seldom read except by research specialists, seminary professors, or their students who are given assignments in this field.

When these volumes are consulted, it is almost always for the light the writings throw on early church history, and in particular on the emergence of new developments in ecclesiastical structure and doctrine. Occasionally, attention is directed to what is indicated of the preaching or liturgy of public worship in this period. Yet what these writings reveal of the personal Christian faith, the wise counsel on perennial human problems, and the devotional life of these various authors has been largely bypassed.

Yet it was precisely this personal faith and devotion which sustained the early Christians in the difficult days of transition which followed the death of Paul, of Peter, and of the other first-century apostles. Having as yet developed only the bare outlines of structure and doctrine, the church could have foundered without the undergirding power of the Holy Spirit in the lives of its leaders and members.

From general oversight, the devotional writings which lie just beyond the close of the biblical canon, and in some cases in books which came very near being included in the Bible, are largely unfamiliar. Yet there is much there that can speak to us in our time—golden treasure waiting to be mined. What this book attempts to do is simply to assay the ore to disclose the nuggets.

One may ask, "How could anything written so long ago in a very different world have anything to say to us today?" Equally well this question might be asked about the Bible, and is being asked. Yet in spite of a different setting, no informed Christian doubts the relevance of the major notes in the biblical message. What is included in these devotional writings from the early years lies just over the line chronologically from the New Testament writings, and sprang from the same life-transforming faith in the coming of God to man in Jesus Christ his Son and our Savior.

Admittedly, the word "devotional" is an ambiguous term. The guiding principle in what is included among these selections is simply that a passage contain an enduring message of Christian faith to the human spirit and thus have relevance to the life of today. The reader will find moving prayers, though prayer is not the major note of the compilation, numerous excerpts from letters of counsel, martyrdoms and glorious spiritual triumph, apocalypse, allegory, moral injunction, and great poetry. One may take his choice!

Naturally we shall not expect to find in these writings anything about science, technology, the nuclear-space age, or various other aspects of the modern world. Yet in spite of difference there is more than a little similarity between the social and religious setting of these writings and our own time. Christianity was on the defensive then; it must renew itself or go under today. There were "gods many and lords many" in those days; amid various forms of idolatry and a pervasive secular humanism we too can say with those early Christians, "Yet for us there is one God, the Father, from whom are all things and for whom we exist, and one Lord, Jesus Christ, through whom are all things and through whom we exist" (I Cor. 8:6). The early Christian community had often to choose between their loyalty to God and the power of the state; so must we. There was persecution and political upheaval then; there is now, and to our sorrow we have had to learn that martyrdom, often in tragic proportions, is not a thing of the past.

In short, those were dark days, yet glorious with the light of faith. Those early Christians did not possess more than a fragment of our present knowledge, yet they had a deep wisdom of the heart. This fact has prompted a recent writer to remark, "Psychological and sociological insights as keen or keener than anything the modern world slickly sells may be found in the parables of ancient rabbis and the homilies of early church fathers." [1]

A word may be in order as to the relation of these writings to the Bible. A little examination will make it evident that the selections deal with many of the same themes. In individual passages the way the theme is presented may be more or less arresting than the words of the Bible. Comparisons are indicated for those who wish to pursue them. Yet there is no intention in presenting these selections to

[1] Edwin Scott Gaustad, *A Religious History of America* (New York: Harper & Row, 1966), p. 391.

make them a substitute for the Bible. As a whole, the wisdom of the selection of those books which form the canon of the Bible has been demonstrated by the test of time. But in a vital way these other writings supplement the Bible. If the essential mark of inspiration is the power to inspire, then these too may be regarded as inspired if they move us to deeper adoration, trust, thanksgiving, and commitment to the call of God.

How should this anthology be used? In compiling it I have anticipated several major uses, which may determine the mood and manner in which it should be read.

One procedure is to read the excerpts simply as one would any other significant writing from the past, for the interest they elicit or the information they give. There are important things disclosed here about the life and times and modes of thought of the early church. Some of these matters are pointed out in the brief introductions; others are evident to the observing in the passages themselves.

A second possible use is as a manual of personal devotions on a mature level. No one knows how many people continue the practice of daily devotional reading and prayer. Yet certainly many do, for devotional guides keep coming from the presses. Some of these are of enduring value; others are ephemeral if not superficial. The selections in this anthology, read one at a time and thought about with discernment and personal application, can be the basis of fruitful Christian reflection. With each a related Bible reading is suggested for those who wish to combine these sources.

Still a third use is to supplement the more familiar devotional classics for reading in spiritual retreats. It is becoming more and more common to withdraw from ordinary activities for a day, a weekend, or a longer period to find spiritual renewal in company with others of similar intention. In this compilation can be found inspirational material not generally known or easily available elsewhere.

A fourth objective incorporates the preceding but with a distinctive turn. This is the furtherance of ecumenical worship, and hence of a more vital ecumenism within the currents of our time. In short, it aims to be an instrument of "spiritual training" for Christians of all the many households of faith. The early church had its own sources of division, against which these writings repeatedly warn, but there were as yet no denominations in the modern sense. Hence, these words can speak equally to all of us in our time.

Still a fifth use could be the enrichment of public worship in the churches of today. Not all the passages would be appropriate to the same degree, but for this purpose the personal and liturgical prayers found in First Clement, the Martyrdom of Polycarp, and the Didache might be especially apt, and the little-known but moving poetry of the so-called Odes of Solomon constitutes a psalter of majestic beauty.

The selections have been arranged chronologically as nearly as it is possible to date them, with the exception of placing the martyrdom of Polycarp along with his letter and the excerpts from the book of poetry at the end. Since each one stems from the author's life and thought, a note in regard to what is known of his life and of the date, place, and purpose of writing introduces each division. There is also a brief note to introduce each passage selected for inclusion. I am alone responsible for the titles.

At the end of the Gospel of John we read, "But there are also many other things which Jesus did; were every one of them to be written, I suppose that the world itself could not contain the books that would be written." The proliferation of writing stemming from the deeds and words of Jesus continues to the present without diminution. The writings presented in this compilation do not throw any new light on the life story of the man of Nazareth or make possible a new biography. What they do indicate is what the Spirit of Christ was saying to Christ's followers in those momentous early days. And is it unreasonable to suppose that this same Spirit can speak to us through their words today?

First Clement

The earliest Christian writing which has come down to us from outside the New Testament is a long letter from the church at Rome to the church at Corinth. It contains sixty-five sections or chapters, and so is hardly a letter in the usual sense, but it is obviously addressed as a message from one church group to another. It does not bear the author's name, but a very early and probably reliable tradition ascribes it to a leader of the Roman church by the name of Clement. He has come to be known in the Catholic church as St. Clement, an early successor to St. Peter.

It is not certain just who this Clement was.

While he has long been regarded as the third, or possibly the fourth, Bishop of Rome, it is doubtful that by his time a clear distinction had been drawn between bishops and presbyters, or elders, or that a definite episcopal succession had yet been established. From the nature of his writing it seems probable that he was a very able Hellenistic Jew who had been converted to the Christian faith and had risen to the position of being a leading, and quite likely *the* leading, presbyter-bishop of the Roman church. In that capacity it was natural that he should write in the name of the congregation to a sister church located at Corinth.

Whoever Clement may have been, he was thoroughly saturated with the Old Testament scriptures, from which he quotes extensively. He was also familiar with the writings of Paul, especially I Corinthians, which he somewhat uses as a model for his own letter. He says much of Jesus but quotes him very little, which may indicate that he was not familiar with the Gospels. He was deeply concerned about the moral life of the Christian and gives many wholesome injunctions in regard to it, and he appears to have been more impressed than Paul was with the disclosure of God in the world of nature. Viewing his writing as a whole, one may judge that he was a devout, intelligent, and committed Christian who was deeply concerned both with the gospel of Christ and with the effectiveness of the church as its witness and carrier.

The occasion which evoked the letter was not unlike that which earlier had prompted Paul to write to the Corinthian church. Some younger men had apparently rebelled against the authority of their older leaders and had succeeded in deposing the ruling presbyters. Revolt is nothing new in either church or society! We do not know with certainty what the fuss was about, but there are hints that the rebels thought they had spiritual gifts (possibly speaking in tongues) and superior secret knowledge (*gnosis*) not adequately appreciated by the elder statesmen.

Which faction was right we do not know, and had we been present we might have judged that there was right and wrong on both sides. Clement, however, was a strong advocate of law and order, and he wrote to rebuke the dissidents. At the same time, he believed it essential to "maintain the unity of the Spirit in the bond of peace" (Eph. 4:3) and his plea for harmony in the church of Christ contains an eloquent tribute to love which much resembles that of Paul in his first letter to the Corinthians.

When did Clement write this letter? It is undated except as the time can be discerned from its contents, but is usually believed to have been written in the last decade of the first century of the Christian era. The letter was being sent by trustworthy and discreet persons who from youth to old age lived irreproachable Christian lives. The persecutions under Nero, which had occurred in A.D. 64, were past, but references to fresh persecutions probably refer to those under the emperor Domitian. This is the primary clue to its date as A.D. 96 or 97.

If this date is approximately correct, it is evident that this writing antedates several books of the New Testament which are believed to have been written after the turn of the century, notably I and II Timothy, Titus, James, II Peter, I, II, and III John, and Jude. Why, then, did Clement's letter not find a place in the canon? It almost did. Selections from it along with Paul's letters were read in services of public worship. Clement of Alexandria around the turn of the second century speaks of it as Scripture, and in Egypt and Syria it was regarded as part of the canon. Yet in the winnowing process by which the canon was eventually formed, it probably deserved to be omitted.

Clement's letter to the Corinthians, from which some fragments will be given here, contains some great passages, fully worthy of a place in the New Testament. Yet there are others, particularly those which deal most stringently with the church quarrel which evoked the letter, which do not warm the heart. These serve a useful purpose to the church historian who desires to assess the state of affairs in the churches of Rome and Corinth at the end of the first century. Yet since this is not the purpose in this volume, we shall pass them by.

What, then, does Clement say to the Christian of

today as he endeavors to grow in the life of the Spirit?

1. *Called and Sanctified by the Will of God*

Clement begins his letter with a gracious Christian salutation; then places the rebuke he feels he must give within a warmhearted setting. This selection gives the pattern of what a Christian fellowship ought to be by describing what the church at Corinth was before dissension entered its midst.

The Church of God which sojourns in Rome to the Church of God which sojourns in Corinth, to those who are called and sanctified by the will of God through our Lord Jesus Christ. Grace and peace from God Almighty be multiplied to you through Jesus Christ.

Owing to the sudden and repeated misfortunes and calamities which have befallen us, we consider that our attention has been somewhat delayed in turning to the questions disputed among you, beloved, and especially the abominable and unholy sedition, alien and foreign to the elect of God, which a few rash and self-willed persons have made blaze up to such a frenzy that your name, venerable and famous, and worthy as it is of all men's love, has been much slandered. For who has stayed with you without making proof of the virtue and stedfastness of your faith? who has not admired the sobriety and Christian gentleness of your piety? . . .

23

And you were all humble-minded and in no wise arrogant, yielding subjection rather than demanding it, "giving more gladly than receiving," [1] satisfied with the provision of Christ, and paying attention to his words you stored them up carefully in your hearts, and kept his sufferings before your eyes. Thus a profound and rich peace was given to all, you had an insatiable desire to do good, and the Holy Spirit was poured out in abundance on you all. You were full of holy plans, and with pious confidence you stretched out your hands to Almighty God in a passion of goodness, beseeching him to be merciful towards any unwilling sin. Day and night you strove on behalf of the whole brotherhood that the number of his elect should be saved with mercy and compassion. You were sincere and innocent, and bore no malice to one another. All sedition and all schism was abominable to you. You mourned over the transgressions of your neighbours; you judged their shortcomings as your own. You were without regret in every act of kindness, "ready unto every good work." You were adorned by your virtuous and honourable citizenship and did all things in the fear of God. The commandments and ordinances of the Lord were "written on the tables of your heart."

COMPARE I COR. 1:1-9.

[1] Lake uses quotation marks to indicate indirect as well as direct quotations from the Bible. I have omitted some of them for smoother reading.

2. *God's Gifts of Peace in All Nature*

Clement rebukes the Corinthian church roundly for their jealousies and factions, calling them to repentance and setting before them the example of humility in great figures of the Old Testament such as Abraham, Job, Moses, and David. Then in a beautiful description of the order and harmony of nature he calls them to contemplation of God's "splendid and excellent gifts of peace."

The humility and obedient submission of so many men of such great fame, have rendered better not only us, but also the generations before us, who received his oracles in fear and truth. Seeing then that we have received a share in many great and glorious deeds, let us hasten on to the goal of peace, which was given us from the beginning, and let us fix our gaze on the Father and Creator of the whole world and cleave to his splendid and excellent gifts of peace, and to his good deeds to us. Let us contemplate him with our mind, let us gaze with the eyes of our soul on his long-suffering purpose, let us consider how free from wrath he is towards all his creatures.

The heavens moving at his appointment are subject to him in peace; day and night follow the course allotted by him without hindering each other. Sun and moon and the companies of the stars roll on, according to his direction, in harmony, in their appointed courses, and swerve not from them at all. The earth teems according to his will at its proper seasons, and puts forth food in full abundance for men and beasts and all the living things that are on it, with no dissension, and changing none of his decrees. . . . The hollow of the boundless sea is gathered by his working into its allotted places, and does not pass the barriers placed around it, but does even as he enjoined on it; for he said "Thus far shalt thou come, and thy waves shall be broken within thee." The ocean, which men cannot pass, and the worlds beyond it, are ruled by the same injunctions of the Master. The seasons of spring, summer, autumn, and winter give place to one another in peace. The stations of the winds fulfil their service without hindrance at the proper time. The everlasting springs, created for enjoyment and health, supply sustenance for the life of man without fail; and the smallest of animals meet together in concord and peace. All these things did the great Creator and Master of the universe ordain to be in peace and concord, and to all things does he do good, and more especially to us who have fled for refuge to his mercies through our Lord Jesus Christ, to whom be the glory and the majesty for ever and ever. Amen.

COMPARE Ps. 104:1-24.

3. *One Body in Christ*

Clement was one of the first to draw a distinction between clergy and laity in the church and to claim

26

apostolic authority for the former. Yet as strongly as
Paul he believed in the need for every member of the
Christian fellowship to respect and serve one another
in humility and love.

Let us therefore, brethren, campaign most stren-
uously under his faultless orders. Let us observe
those who campaign under our rulers,—with what
discipline, subordination, and obedience they exe-
cute their orders. They are not all generals or colo-
nels or captains or lieutenants, and so forth, but
each one in his own rank carries out the orders
given by the emperor and the rulers. The great cannot exist without the small, nor the small without
the great. There is a kind of blending among all,
and there is an advantage in that. Let us take our
body; the head is nothing without the feet, just as
the feet are nothing without the head. The smallest
parts of our body are necessary and useful to the
whole body. But they all coalesce and experience a
common submission, in order to preserve the whole
body.

So let our whole body be preserved through
Christ Jesus, and let each one be subject to his
neighbor, as he has been placed by his spiritual
gift. Let the strong care for the weak, and let the
weak respect the strong. Let the rich provide for
the poor, and let the poor give thanks to God, because he has given him one to supply his need. Let
the wise man show his wisdom not in words but

in good deeds. Let the humble-minded not bear witness to himself, but let himself have witness borne to him by others. Let him that is pure in the flesh not boast of it, knowing that it is another who bestows on him his self-control. So let us consider, brethren, of what matter we were made, who we are, and what kind of beings we came into the world, from what a dark grave he that formed and created us brought us into his world, where he had prepared his benefits for us before we were born. Since therefore we have received all this from him we ought to give him thanks for everything. To him be glory forever and ever! Amen.

COMPARE I COR. 12:4-27.

4. *In Praise of Love*

Though Clement did not hesitate to rebuke the Corinthians for quarreling and rebelling against authority, his main approach was a call to love one another with a love grounded in the love of God. Note how this passage reflects the spirit of I Corinthians 13, with which he was, of course, familiar, since Paul's letters had been widely circulated among the churches.

Let him who has love in Christ perform the commandments of Christ. Who is able to explain the bond of the love of God? Who is sufficient to tell the greatness of its beauty? The height to which love lifts us is not to be expressed. Love unites us to God. "Love covereth a multitude of sins. Love beareth all things, is long-suffering in all things. There is nothing base, nothing haughty in love; love admits no schism, love makes no sedition, love does all things in concord. In love were all the elect of God made perfect. Without love is nothing well pleasing to God. In love did the Master receive us; for the sake of the love which he had towards us did Jesus Christ our Lord give his blood by the will of God for us, and his flesh for our flesh, and his soul for our souls."

See, beloved, how great and wonderful is love, and that of its perfection there is no expression. Who is able to be found in it save those to whom God grants it? Let us then beg and pray of his mercy that we may be found in love, without human partisanship, free from blame. . . . Blessed are we, beloved, if we perform the commandments of God in the concord of love, that through love our sins may be forgiven. For it is written "Blessed are they whose iniquities are forgiven, and whose sins are covered; blessed is the man whose sin the Lord will not reckon, and in whose mouth is no guile." This blessing was given to those who have been chosen by God through Jesus Christ our Lord, to whom be the glory for ever and ever. Amen.

Compare I Corinthians 13.

5. *A Pastoral Prayer*

Clement closes his letter of admonition with a pastoral prayer so rich in adoration, so moving in intercession, that it could well be spoken to our need today.

Grant us to hope on thy name, the source of all creation, open the eyes of our heart to know thee, that thou alone art the highest in the highest and remainest holy among the holy. Thou dost humble the pride of the haughty, thou dost destroy the imaginings of nations, thou dost raise up the humble and abase the lofty, thou makest rich and makest poor, thou dost slay and make alive, thou alone art the finder of spirits and art God of all flesh, thou dost look on the abysses, thou seest into the works of man, thou art the helper of those in danger, the saviour of those in despair, the creator and watcher over every spirit; thou dost multiply nations upon earth and hast chosen out from them all those that love thee through Jesus Christ thy beloved child, and through him hast thou taught us, made us holy, and brought us to honour.

We beseech thee, Master, to be our help and succour. Save those of us who are in affliction, have mercy on the lowly, raise the fallen, show thyself to those in need, heal the sick, turn again the wanderers of thy people, feed the hungry, ransom our prisoners, raise up the weak, comfort the faint-hearted; let all "nations know thee, that thou art God alone," and that Jesus Christ is thy child, and

30

that "we are thy people and the sheep of thy pasture."

For thou through thy operations didst make manifest the eternal fabric of the world; thou, Lord, didst create the earth. Thou that art faithful in all generations, righteous in judgment, wonderful in strength and majesty, wise in thy creation, and prudent in establishing thy works, good in the things which are seen, and gracious among those that trust in thee, O merciful and compassionate, forgive us our iniquities and unrighteousness, and transgressions, and shortcomings. Reckon not every sin of thy servants and handmaids, but cleanse us with the cleansing of thy truth, and "guide our steps to walk in holiness of heart, to do the things which are good and pleasing before thee" and before our rulers. Yea, Lord, "make thy face to shine upon us" in peace for our good that we may be sheltered by thy mighty hand, and delivered from all sin by thy uplifted arm, and deliver us from them that hate us wrongfully. Give concord and peace to us and to all that dwell on the earth, as thou didst give to our fathers who called on thee in holiness with faith and truth, and grant that we may be obedient to thy almighty and glorious name, and to our rulers and governors upon the earth.

Thou, Master, hast given the power of sovereignty to them through thy excellent and inexpressible might, that we may know the glory and honour given to them by thee, and be subject to them, in nothing resisting thy will. And to them, Lord, grant health, peace, concord, firmness that they may administer the government which thou hast given them without offence. For thou, heavenly Master, king of eternity, hast given to the sons of men glory and honour and power over the things which are on the earth; do thou, O Lord, direct their counsels according to that which is good and pleasing before thee, that they may administer with piety in peace and gentleness the power given to them by thee, and may find mercy in thine eyes. O thou who alone art able to do these things and far better things for us, we praise thee through Jesus Christ, the high priest and guardian of our souls, through whom be glory and majesty to thee, both now and for all generations and for ever and ever. Amen.

COMPARE PSALM 33.

6. *Blessing and Doxology*

The letter ends on a very personal, yet a universal, note. The names of the messengers would never have been heard of save for their inclusion here; yet the need to bear the good news of harmony and fellowship in Christ is as vital in the twentieth century as the first. Here ecumenicity begins.

Now may God, the all-seeing, and the master of spirits, and the Lord of all flesh, who chose out the Lord Jesus Christ, and us through him for "a peculiar people," give unto every soul that is called after his glorious and holy name, faith, fear, peace, patience and long-suffering, self-control, purity, sobriety, that they may be well-pleasing to his name through our high priest and guardian Jesus Christ, through whom be to him glory and majesty, might and honour, both now and to all eternity. Amen.

Send back quickly to us our messengers Claudius Ephebus and Valerius Vito and Fortunatus, in peace with gladness, in order that they may report the sooner the peace and concord which we pray for and desire, that we also may the more speedily rejoice in your good order.

The grace of our Lord Jesus Christ be with you and with all, in every place, who have been called by God through him, through whom be to him glory, honour, power and greatness and eternal dominion, from eternity to eternity. Amen.

COMPARE ROM. 16:17-27.

Ignatius

We come now to a writing which is of a quite different mood and flavor from that of Clement. Instead of moving along with a steady, calm exaltation of spirit, this writing is fiery, staccato, full of arresting metaphors, and leaping from point to point with abrupt transitions. Had the words been spoken instead of written, they would be considered eloquent, though it is probable that the hearers would catch the speaker's mood more readily than an outline of what he said.

There is a reason for this. Like any such writing it reflects the spirit and convictions of the author.

Yet there is a particular reason for its tenor in the circumstances under which it was written.

Ignatius was Bishop of Antioch in Syria, the same Antioch in which some seventy years earlier those of the Way had first been called Christians and where Paul under the tutelage of Barnabas had begun his ministry (Acts 11:19-26). A strong church from the beginning, it had apparently continued to be one of the major centers of the Christian faith. While in the New Testament writings and in Clement there seems to be no clear differentiation between the offices of bishop and presbyter, the situation had changed by the second decade of the second Christian century. Each church had a bishop of its own along with presbyters and deacons, although the diocesan system had not yet emerged. Ignatius had risen to this place of leadership in Antioch, and he was so convinced that the fidelity of the church required loyalty and obedience to the bishop that this note appears repeatedly in his writing.

Toward the end of the reign of the emperor Trajan, who died in 117, a persecution arose which involved the church at Antioch. As a result its bishop was condemned to the fate of being taken to Rome chained to Roman guards, there to be executed by being thrown to the lions in the Colosseum. There is no record of specific charges against Ignatius, though from his tendency to speak his mind he may have offended the Roman authorities.

35

In any case, as leader of the church he took the brunt of the opposition.

The route taken was overland through Asia Minor, first with a halt at Philadelphia and then with a probably longer stop at Smyrna, on the Aegean coast. Here he was welcomed by Polycarp, the young Bishop of Smyrna whose own martyrdom forty years later will be considered in a later section. Delegations from the neighboring churches of Ephesus, Magnesia, and Tralles, including respectively their bishops Onesimus, Damas, and Polybius, also came to see Ignatius. In Smyrna, Ignatius was permitted to write and dispatch four letters, one to each of the three churches that had sent representatives to greet him and a fourth to Rome. Getting their titles from these places, they are known as the letters to the Ephesians, Magnesians, Trallians, and Romans.

Moving northward, Ignatius and his guards stopped again at Troas. From this point he wrote letters of warm appreciation and judicious counsel to the churches of Philadelphia and Smyrna, where he had stopped on the way, with a brief personal note to Polycarp. From a later writing by Polycarp it appears that Ignatius made one more stop, at Philippi, where his fellow Christians welcomed him with brotherly love. Here he dropped out of sight, though it is probable that he was martyred at Rome in the expected manner. There are indications in his letters to the Philadelphians and to Polycarp that even before he reached Troas the persecutions at Antioch had ceased, but this seems not to have saved him.

The seven letters survived as the legacy of Ignatius to posterity. Written as they were under sentence of death, they must be judged accordingly. Often they have not been, and from the passage in the letter to the Romans in which he describes in gory detail his impending death, urging his fellow Christians at Rome to do nothing to prevent it, he has been charged with sheer masochism. Admittedly, this is contrary to the normative pattern of the Christian faith, both in the early church and at present. For this reason I have omitted it. Yet in it one can detect not only a resolute desire to follow in the steps of his Lord at any cost, but also a genuine humility. Indeed, it is possible that Ignatius' bold assertions were due to an inner lack of boldness, for he repeatedly asks his fellow Christians to pray for him. In any case, this passage should not overshadow the deeply Christian spirit revealed elsewhere in Ignatius' letters.

Excerpts will be cited topically rather than consecutively, and will consist mainly of some of the author's pungent statements about the nature and requirements of the Christian life. No attempt will be made to indicate the frequency of his injunctions to obey the bishop, but since these are interwoven with other fine passages, some examples will be given. The same may be said of his warnings against heresy, which are the occasion for an affirmation of the true humanity of Jesus which antedates the Apostles' Creed and suggests its emphases. Numerous passages reveal both strife and close-knit fellowship in the early church, and it is significant that Ignatius was the first to use the term "catholic" in regard to it. The excerpts will conclude with an indication of how Ignatius' sense of mission in his martyrdom is interwoven with tender statements of brotherly concern and deep gratitude toward those who have supported him in his trials.

1. *Of Faith and Love*

Addressing the church at Ephesus with great affection, Ignatius states his joy in their fidelity, gives his own credentials as a humble follower of Christ, and exhorts them to faith and love as befits the Christian. The term "Theophorus," which means "the God-bearer," is probably an honorary title which indicates the esteem in which Ignatius was held.

Ignatius, who is also called Theophorus, to the Church, worthy of all felicitation, which is at Ephesus in Asia,—blessed with greatness by the fulness of God the Father, predestined from eternity for abiding and unchangeable glory, united and chosen through true suffering by the will of the Father and Jesus Christ our God,—abundant greeting in Jesus Christ and in blameless joy. . . .

I do not give you commands as if I were some one great, for though I am a prisoner for the Name, I am not yet perfect in Jesus Christ; for now I do but begin to be a disciple, and I speak to you as to my fellow learners. For I needed to be prepared by you in faith, exhortation, endurance, long-suffering. But since love does not suffer me to be silent concerning you, for this reason I have taken upon me to exhort you that you live in harmony with the will of God. For Jesus Christ, our inseparable life, is the will of the Father, even as the bishops, who have been appointed throughout the world, are by the will of Jesus Christ. . . .

I have learnt, however, that some from elsewhere have stayed with you, who have evil doctrine; but you did not suffer them to sow it among you, and stopped your ears, so that you might not receive what they sow, seeing that you are as stones of the temple of the Father, . . . carried up to the heights by the engine of Jesus Christ, that is the cross, and using as a rope the Holy Spirit. And your faith is your windlass and love is the road which leads up to God. You are then all fellow travellers, and carry with you God, and the Temple, and Christ, and holiness, and are in all ways adorned by commandments of Jesus Christ. And I share in this joy, for it has been granted to me to speak to you through my writing, and to rejoice with you, that you love nothing, according to human life, but God alone. . . .

None of these things are unknown to you if you possess perfect faith towards Jesus Christ, and love, which are the beginning and end of life;

for the beginning is faith and the end is love, and when the two are joined together in unity it is God, and all other noble things follow after them. No man who professes faith sins, nor does he hate who has obtained love. "The tree is known by its fruits"; so they who profess to be of Christ shall be seen by their deeds. For the deed is not in present profession, but is shown by the power of faith, if a man continue to the end.

COMPARE GAL. 5:6, 13-15, 22-24.

2. *Of Speech and Silence*

Ignatius here continues with counsel as to the importance to the Christian of actions which speak louder than words. His reference to the speech and silence of Jesus is a graphic expression of the authenticity of the total life of Jesus, but it may also have special reference to Jesus' silence at his own trial.

It is better to keep quiet and be real, than to chatter and be unreal. It is a good thing to teach if, that is, the teacher practices what he preaches. There was one such Teacher, who "spoke and it was done"; and what he did in silence is worthy of the Father. He who has really grasped what Jesus said can appreciate his silence. Thus he will be perfect: his words will mean action, and his very silence will reveal his character.

The Lord overlooks nothing. Even secrets are open to him. Let us, then, do everything as if he

were dwelling in us. Thus we shall be his temples
and he will be within us as our God—as he actually
is. This will be clear to us just to the extent that
we love him rightly.

COMPARE MATT. 27:11-14; HEB. 4:11-13.

3. *There Is Nothing Better than Peace*

Ignatius here exhorts his fellow Christians to prayer
for others and to a magnanimous spirit under attack,
such as befits the followers of Christ. The resulting
harmony is furthered by common worship.

Pray constantly for other men, also, for in their
case there is a hope of repentance, that they may
find God. Permit them to be instructed by you, at
least through your deeds. To their anger, be meek;
to their boasts, be humble; to their abuse, utter your
prayers; to their error, be steadfast in faith; to their
savagery, be gentle; not zealous to imitate them. Let
us show ourselves their brothers by forbearance, and
let us be zealous to imitate the Lord, to see who
can be more wronged, defrauded, set at naught, so
that no plant of the devil may be found in you,
but with all purity and sobriety you may remain in
union with Jesus Christ, in both flesh and spirit. . . .

So be zealous to meet together more frequently
to give thanks to God and glorify him. For when
you meet together frequently, Satan's powers are
destroyed and his destructiveness comes to naught

through the harmony of your faith. There is nothing better than peace, by which every war of beings in heaven or on earth is nullified.

COMPARE ROM. 12:9-21.

4. *One in Christ and the Bishop*

Greatly concerned to preserve the unity of the church, Ignatius held this unity to be centered not only in Christ but ecclesiastically in the bishop. Unlike Clement, who attributed the bishop's authority to apostolic succession, Ignatius thought of the bishop as being God's direct representative. Yet the bishop is himself a fallible person in need of divine help, as is evident both from Ignatius' frequent acknowledgments of his own need of the prayers of the church and from his words of counsel, cited in the second excerpt, to his younger colleague Polycarp.

Therefore it is fitting that you should live in harmony with the will of the bishop, as indeed you do. For your justly famous presbytery, worthy of God, is attuned to the bishop as the strings to a harp. Therefore by your concord and harmonious love Jesus Christ is being sung. Now do each of you join in this choir, that being harmoniously in concord you may receive the key of God in unison, and sing with one voice through Jesus Christ to the Father, that he may both hear you and may recognise, through your good works, that you are members of his Son. It is therefore profitable for you to

42

be in blameless unity, in order that you may always commune with God. . . .

Ignatius, who is also called Theophorus, to Polycarp, who is bishop of the Church of the Smyrnaeans, or rather has for his bishop God the Father and the Lord Jesus Christ, abundant greeting.

Welcoming your godly mind which is fixed as if on immovable rock, I glory exceedingly that it was granted me to see your blameless face wherein I would fain have pleasure in God. I exhort you to press forward on your course, in the grace wherewith you are endued, and to exhort all men to gain salvation. Vindicate your office with all diligence, both of the flesh and spirit. Care for unity, for there is nothing better. Help all men, as the Lord also helps you; suffer all men in love, as you indeed do. Be diligent with unceasing prayer. Entreat for wisdom greater than you have, be watchful and keep the spirit from slumbering. Speak to each individually after the manner of God. Bear the sicknesses of all as a perfect athlete. Where the toil is greatest, is the gain great.

If you love good disciples, it is no credit to you; rather bring to subjection by your gentleness the more troublesome. Not all wounds are healed by the same plaster. Relieve convulsions by fomentations. "Be prudent as the serpent" in all things and "pure as the dove" for ever. For this reason you consist of flesh and spirit, that you may deal tenderly with the things which appear visibly; but pray

43

that the invisible things may be revealed to you, that you may lack nothing and abound in every gift. The time calls on you to attain unto God, just as pilots require wind, and the storm-tossed sailor seeks a harbour. Be sober as God's athlete. The prize is immortality and eternal life, of which you have been persuaded. In all things I am devoted to you,—I and my bonds, which you loved.

COMPARE EPH. 4:1-7, 11-16; TITUS 1:5-9.

5. *One Altar, One Eucharist*

Baptism and the Lord's Supper were already sacred rites of the church by the time Ignatius wrote, and he attached great importance to them both as channels of divine grace and as bonds of unity with one another and with Christ. This has significant bearing on the ecumenical movement today.

If Jesus Christ permit me through your prayers, and it be his will, in the second book, which I propose to write to you,[1] I will show you concerning the dispensation of the new man Jesus Christ, which I have begun to discuss, dealing with his faith and his love, his suffering and his resurrection; especially if the Lord reveal to me that you all severally join in the common meeting in grace from his name, in one faith and in Jesus Christ, "who

[1] This second book was never written.

44

was of the family of David according to the flesh," the Son of Man and the Son of God, so that you obey the bishop and the presbytery with an undisturbed mind, breaking one bread, which is the medicine of immortality, the antidote that we should not die, but live for ever in Jesus Christ. . . .

Be careful therefore to use one Eucharist (for there is one flesh of our Lord Jesus Christ, and one cup for union with his blood, one altar, as there is one bishop with the presbytery and the deacons my fellow servants), in order that whatever you do you may do it according unto God. . . .

Let your baptism remain as your arms, your faith as your helmet, your love as a spear, your endurance as your panoply, let your works be your deposits that you may receive the back-pay due to you. Be therefore long-suffering with one another in gentleness, as God is with you. May I have joy in you always.

COMPARE I COR. 11:23-26; EPH. 6:10-17.

6. *One Faith*

By the time of Ignatius' death the heresy of docetism, which denied the real humanity of Jesus, had emerged. Ignatius strongly opposed this view and made his own self-offering dependent on the incarnation, though he does not use this term. In his affirmations of the true manhood of Jesus he uses words which in some measure anticipate the later formulation of the Apostles' Creed.

Be deaf, then, to any talk that ignores Jesus Christ, of David's lineage, of Mary; who was really born, ate, and drank; was really persecuted under Pontius Pilate; was really crucified and died, in the sight of heaven and earth and the underworld. He was really raised from the dead, for his Father raised him, just as his Father will raise us, who believe on him, through Christ Jesus, apart from whom we have no genuine life.

And if, as some atheists (I mean unbelievers) say, his suffering was a sham (it's really *they* who are a sham!), why, then, am I a prisoner? Why do I want to fight with wild beasts? In that case I shall die to no purpose. Yes, and I am maligning the Lord too!

Flee, then, these wicked offshoots which produce deadly fruit. If a man taste of it, he dies outright. They are none of the Father's planting. For had they been, they would have shown themselves as branches of the cross, and borne immortal fruit. It is through the cross, by his suffering, that he summons you who are his members. A head cannot be born without limbs, since God stands for unity. It is his nature.

COMPARE JOHN 1:14-18; I COR. 15:12-19.

7. *Jesus Christ the Word*

This significant passage gives evidence that debate about the authority of scripture is nothing new in the

46

church! Ignatius answers the argument on the same ground to which we must appeal today—the "inviolable archives" of the coming of Jesus Christ, his death and resurrection, and the faith that came by him to be held in love.

I urge you, do not do things in cliques, but act as Christ's disciples. When I heard some people saying, "If I don't find it in the original documents, I don't believe it in the gospel," I answered them, "But it *is* written there." They retorted, "That's just the question." To my mind it is Jesus Christ who is the original documents. The inviolable archives are his cross and death and his resurrection and the faith that came by him. It is by these things and through your prayers that I want to be justified.

Priests are a fine thing, but better still is the High Priest who was entrusted with the Holy of Holies. He alone was entrusted with God's secrets. He is the door to the Father. Through it there enter Abraham, Isaac, and Jacob, the prophets and apostles and the Church. All these find their place in God's unity. But there is something special about the gospel—I mean the coming of the Saviour, our Lord Jesus Christ, his Passion and resurrection. The beloved prophets announced his coming; but the gospel is the crowning achievement forever. All these things, taken together, have their value, provided you hold the faith in love.

COMPARE I COR. 1:18-31.

8. *Farewell in Jesus Christ*

In these words of farewell there is a tenderness in the thought of Ignatius which is in marked contrast with his apparent eagerness for martyrdom as expressed in his more familiar letter to the Romans. Yet may it not be that this tenderness complements rather than contradicts the passionate devotion of the latter?

I send you greetings from Smyrna, as do the churches of God that are with me, who have rested me in body and spirit. My chains exhort you, which I carry around with me for the sake of Jesus Christ, praying that I may reach the presence of God; continue to be harmonious and to pray with one another. For it is right that every one of you, and particularly the elders, should cheer the bishop, in honor of the Father and of Jesus Christ and the apostles. I pray that you may listen to me in love, so that I may not by having written become evidence against you. But pray for me too, for I need your love, by the mercy of God, so that I may be found worthy to obtain the lot which it is incumbent upon me to obtain, so that I may not be disqualified.

The love of the Smyrnaeans and Ephesians greets you. Remember in your prayers the church in Syria, in which I am not worthy to be counted, for I am the least of them. Farewell in Jesus Christ. . . . Love one another every one of you with undivided heart. My spirit offers itself for you not only now, but also when I shall reach the presence of God. For I am still in danger, but through Jesus Christ the Father can be counted on to answer my prayer and yours. May you be found faultless in union with him.

COMPARE PHIL. 1:1-21.

Polycarp

We come now to Polycarp, Bishop of Smyrna, to
whom we have already been introduced through
the letters of Ignatius. Since he was martyred in
155 or 156, and in his noble word in defense of his
faith before the proconsul states his age as eighty-
six, he must have been in his mid-forties at the
time he extended the hand of Christian fellowship
to Ignatius on his road to martyrdom.

Only one letter of Polycarp's has been preserved.
This was written to the church at Philippi in Mace-
donia soon after Ignatius had passed through and
before any word of his fate had been received. The

occasion was a reply to the Philippian church, which had asked for copies of Ignatius' letters. Polycarp sent them with a covering letter, the purpose of which is indicated in the words, "We are sending you the letters of Ignatius, those he addressed to us and any others we had by us, just as you requested. They are herewith appended to this letter."

While the excerpts in this anthology are in general arranged chronologically as nearly as they can be dated, an exception is made in the account of the martyrdom of Polycarp, which is dated some forty years later than his letter to the Philippians. This moving and dramatic story is contained in a letter from the church of Smyrna to the church of Philomelium, two hundred miles to the east. Its ending states that Gaius copied it from the papers of Irenaeus, a disciple of Polycarp, and that a certain Pontius copied it again from Gaius' copy when it was almost worn out with age. However, its authorship is uncertain.

Whoever the original author may have been, it is not only a skillfully told but a highly significant story. It is the first detailed account of a martyrdom that we have outside the New Testament. Besides paying tribute to a man who seems to have been of an unusually saintly character, it suggests the beginnings of a veneration of the saints. That it was sent to a church of no great renown, one that was not a prominent center like Ephesus or Rome, shows something of the range to which the church had spread by the middle of the second century. Eusebius thought this account worthy of inclusion in his annals, from which it is chiefly known, though he omitted, as we shall, some of its more miraculous elements.

It is from this one letter of Polycarp's and the account of his death, plus the tributes of Ignatius and the fact that Irenaeus was proud to regard him as his teacher, that we glean what we know of Polycarp. However, these sources are enough to indicate that he was an able administrator and a humble, discerning, deeply dedicated Christian, no great genius or skilled writer, but much beloved for what he was.

Polycarp's letter is saturated with quotations from what was later to be called the New Testament, which indicates that these manuscripts had already been circulated widely in the churches and that he had read them faithfully. There are quotations from the first three Gospels (though not from the fourth), from Acts, from Paul's letters to the churches with numerous references to "the blessed Paul," and from Timothy, Hebrews, James, I Peter, and I and II John. There are also allusions to the letters of Clement and Ignatius. From this assembling of quotations Polycarp has been sometimes regarded as lacking in originality, but one may also pay tribute to him for being so versed in great writings which were later to become scripture. In fact, he was the first writer to refer to a passage from the New Testament as scripture, as he does in quoting from Eph. 4:26 (Letter to the Philippians 12).

In 154 or 155, shortly before his martyrdom, Polycarp made the long journey to Rome to try to reach an agreement with the bishop Anicetus as to the proper date for the observance of Easter. Already the eastern and western branches of the church had different dates for its observance, as they do even today. He did not succeed, but Polycarp and Anicetus parted friends in a spirit of mutual goodwill. That this could occur when Polycarp was already in his eighties shows something about both his physical and his spiritual stamina.

Like Ignatius, Polycarp could speak sharply about heretics. Yet in his letter he hardly mentioned Ignatius' recurrent theme of obedience to the bishop, which seems to indicate that he was more concerned with his people's virtuous living than with ecclesiastical authority. The letter consists mainly of good Christian counsel to various groups, among whom he includes wives and widows, the younger men and women, deacons and presbyters. Toward one of the presbyters, Valens, who had been guilty of some dishonesty in money matters, he shows great understanding.

Only two excerpts from Polycarp's letter will be cited, one a sort of summation of his Christian counsel, the other his word of sorrow and compassion regarding Valens. Then at greater length the

53

most crucial passages from the account of his
martyrdom will be included. Note that he dies with
a beautiful prayer on his lips. This is very personal,
yet it contains portions of a liturgy in which he had
many times led his people.

1. *Let Us Hold Constantly to Our Hope*

After giving pastoral counsel to a number of groups
according to their particular needs, Polycarp seems
here to be addressing the entire congregation of the
church at Philippi. The passage contains no literary
flourishes, but it bears the marks of a devoted follower
of Christ who yearns to have his fellow Christians live
uprightly in recollection of the example of Jesus Christ
and the apostles who preceded them.

Let us therefore hold constantly to our hope, and
to the guarantee of our uprightness, that is, Jesus
Christ, who carried the burden of our sins in his
own body on the cross, who committed no sin and
deceit was never on his lips, but he endured it all
for us, so that we might live in union with him. So
let us be imitators of his endurance, and if we suffer for his sake, let us glorify him. For he set us
this example in himself, and this is what we have
believed.

So I beg you all to obey the message of uprightness and to exhibit all endurance, such as you saw
with your own eyes not only in the blessed Igna-

tius and Zosimus and Rufus, but also in others of
your number, and in Paul himself and the rest of
the apostles, being assured that all these have not
run in vain, but in faith and uprightness, and that
they are in the place that they have deserved with
the Lord, with whom they suffered. For they did
not love the present world, but him who died for
us and was raised up by God for our sakes.

So stand fast in these things, and follow the
Lord's example, steadfast in faith and immovable,
loving the brotherhood, devoted to one another,
united in truth, giving way to one another in the
gentleness of the Lord, despising nobody. When
you can do good, do not put it off, for charity de-
livers from death. You must all subordinate yourselves to one another, and live irreproachable lives
among the heathen, so that you may be praised for
your good deeds, and the Lord may not be ill
spoken of through you. But alas for him, on account
of whom the name of the Lord is ill spoken of.
Therefore teach all men to be serious, and be so
yourselves.

COMPARE COL. 1:21-29.

2. *Build One Another Up*

One of the most important marks of a Christian
leader, but difficult to achieve, is found in the ability
to sorrow over the wrong-doing of another without
censoriousness but with no surrender of principle, and
at the same time to turn a bad affair to good account

in the reactions of others. That Polycarp was sufficient-
ly great-hearted to do this is evident from this passage,
which concerns the behavior of a former elder of the
church at Philippi.

I am exceedingly sorry for Valens, who was once
made an elder among you, because he so fails to
understand the position that was given him. I warn
you therefore to abstain from covetousness and to
be pure and truthful. Keep yourselves from all evil.
But how can a man who cannot control himself in
these things preach self-control to someone else?
If a man does not refrain from covetousness, he will
be defiled by idolatry and will be judged as one of
the heathen who are ignorant of the judgment of
the Lord. Or do we not know that God's people are
to be the judges of the world, as Paul teaches?
But I have not found or heard of any such thing
among you, among whom the blessed Paul labored,
and who are mentioned in the beginning of a letter
of his. For he boasts of you in all the churches
which alone had then come to know the Lord; we
had not yet come to know him. Therefore, brethren,
I am very sorry for Valens and for his wife; may
the Lord grant them true repentance! So be self-
controlled in this matter, and do not look on such
people as enemies, but call them back as ailing
members, gone astray, so that you may save your
whole body. For if you do this, you build one another up.

COMPARE GAL. 6:1-10.

POLYCARP

3. *The Martyrdom of Polycarp*

Polycarp seems neither to have courted martyrdom,
as did some of the early Christians, nor to have tried
to evade it. When riots against the Christians broke
out in Smyrna, his friends persuaded him to withdraw to a farm outside the city, and while he was
being sought by the police, he moved to another farm.
However, being betrayed by members of his own
household, he was discovered by the police, from
whom he made no effort to escape. Setting before
them food and drink, he asked only for an hour in
which he might pray undisturbed. His wish being
granted, he prayed for two hours "so filled with the
grace of God" that his captors as well as the bystanders
were much moved and "many repented that they had
come to get such a devout old man." The quoted
excerpt begins at this point.

When at last he had finished his prayer, in which
he remembered all who had met with him at any
time, both small and great, both those with and
those without renown, and the whole Catholic
Church throughout the world, the hour of departure having come, they mounted him on an ass and
brought him into the city. It was a great Sabbath.
And there the chief of the police, Herod, and his
father, Nicetas, met him and transferred him to
their carriage, and tried to persuade him, as they
sat beside him, saying, "What harm is there to say
'Lord Caesar,' and to offer incense and all that sort
of thing, and to save yourself?"

At first he did not answer them. But when they

57

persisted, he said, "I am not going to do what you advise me."

Then when they failed to persuade him, they uttered dire threats and made him get out with such speed that in dismounting from the carriage he bruised his shin. But without turning around, as though nothing had happened, he proceeded swiftly, and was led into the arena, there being such a tumult in the arena that no one could be heard. But as Polycarp was entering the arena, a voice from heaven came to him, saying, "Be strong, Polycarp, and play the man." No one saw the one speaking, but those of our people who were present heard the voice.

And when finally he was brought up, there was a great tumult on hearing that Polycarp had been arrested. Therefore, when he was brought before him, the proconsul asked him if he were Polycarp. And when he confessed that he was, he tried to persuade him to deny [the faith], saying, "Have respect to your age"—and other things that customarily follow this, such as, "Swear by the fortune of Caesar; change your mind; say, 'Away with the atheists!' "

But Polycarp looked with earnest face at the whole crowd of lawless heathen in the arena, and motioned to them with his hand. Then, groaning and looking up to heaven, he said, "Away with the atheists!"

But the proconsul was insistent and said: "Take the oath, and I shall release you. Curse Christ."

Polycarp said: "Eighty-six years I have served him, and he never did me any wrong. How can I blaspheme my King who saved me?"

And upon his persisting still and saying, "Swear by the fortune of Caesar," he answered, "If you vainly suppose that I shall swear by the fortune of Caesar, as you say, and pretend that you do not know who I am, listen plainly: I am a Christian. But if you desire to learn the teaching of Christianity, appoint a day and give me a hearing."

The proconsul said, "Try to persuade the people."

But Polycarp said, "You, I should deem worthy of an account; for we have been taught to render honor, as is befitting, to rulers and authorities appointed by God so far as it does us no harm; but as for these, I do not consider them worthy that I should make defense to them."

But the proconsul said: "I have wild beasts. I shall throw you to them, if you do not change your mind."

But he said: "Call them. For repentance from the better to the worse is not permitted us; but it is noble to change from what is evil to what is righteous."

And again [he said] to him, "I shall have you consumed with fire, if you despise the wild beasts, unless you change your mind."

But Polycarp said: "The fire you threaten burns but an hour and is quenched after a little; for you do not know the fire of the coming judgment and everlasting punishment that is laid up for the impious. But why do you delay? Come, do what you will."

And when he had said these things and many more besides he was inspired with courage and joy, and his face was full of grace, so that not only did it not fall with dismay at the things said to him, but on the contrary, the proconsul was astonished, and sent his own herald into the midst of the arena to proclaim three times: "Polycarp has confessed himself to be a Christian."

When this was said by the herald, the entire crowd of heathen and Jews who lived in Smyrna shouted with uncontrollable anger and a great cry: "This one is the teacher of Asia, the father of the Christians, the destroyer of our gods, who teaches many not to sacrifice nor to worship."

Such things they shouted and asked the Asiarch Philip that he let loose a lion on Polycarp. But he said it was not possible for him to do so, since he had brought the wild-beast sports to a close. Then they decided to shout with one accord that he burn Polycarp alive. For it was necessary that the vision which had appeared to him about his pillow should be fulfilled, when he saw it burning while he was praying, and turning around had said prophetically to the faithful who were with him, "I must be burned alive."

Then these things happened with such dispatch, quicker than can be told—the crowds in so great a hurry to gather wood and faggots from the workshops and the baths, the Jews being especially

zealous, as usual, to assist with this. When the fire
was ready, and he had divested himself of all his
clothes and unfastened his belt, he tried to take off
his shoes, though he was not heretofore in the habit
of doing this because [each of] the faithful always
vied with one another as to which of them would be
first to touch his body. For he had always been
honored, even before his martyrdom, for his holy
life. Straightway then, they set about him the material prepared for the pyre. And when they were
about to nail him also, he said: "Leave me as I am.
For he who grants me to endure the fire will enable
me also to remain on the pyre unmoved, without
the security you desire from the nails."

So they did not nail him, but tied him. And with
his hands put behind him and tied, like a noble
ram out of a great flock ready for sacrifice, a burnt
offering ready and acceptable to God, he looked up
to heaven and said:

"Lord God Almighty, Father of thy beloved and
blessed Servant Jesus Christ, through whom we
have received full knowledge of thee, 'the God of
angels and powers and all creation' and of the
whole race of the righteous who live in thy presence: I bless thee, because thou hast deemed me
worthy of this day and hour, to take my part in the
number of the martyrs, in the cup of thy Christ,
for 'resurrection to eternal life' of soul and body in
the immortality of the Holy Spirit; among whom
may I be received in thy presence this day as a rich

and acceptable sacrifice, just as thou hast prepared and revealed beforehand and fulfilled, thou that art the true God without any falsehood. For this and for everything I praise thee, I bless thee, I glorify thee, through the eternal and heavenly High Priest, Jesus Christ, thy beloved Servant, through whom be glory to thee with him and Holy Spirit both now and unto the ages to come. Amen."

And when he had concluded the Amen and finished his prayer, the men attending to the fire lighted it. . . .

At this point the narrator states that the fire miraculously refused to burn Polycarp's body, making a vaulted chamber about it like a ship's sails filled with wind. An executioner was ordered to stab him with a dagger, whereupon his blood poured forth in such a quantity as to quench the fire. Altercation then followed among the Romans and the Jews over the request of his friends to claim the body of the deceased. The story proper ends with a significant foreshadowing of the future, though the author adds further tributes to Polycarp, greetings in Christ, and a statement of the day and hour of his martyrdom.

The captain of the Jews, when he saw their contentiousness, set it [i.e., his body] in the midst and burned it, as was their custom. So we later took up his bones, more precious than costly stones and more valuable than gold, and laid them away in a suitable place. There the Lord will permit us, so

far as possible, to gather together in joy and gladness to celebrate the day of his martyrdom as a
birthday, in memory of those athletes who have
gone before, and to train and make ready those who
are to come hereafter.

COMPARE ACTS 6:8-15; 7:54-60.

The Shepherd of Hermas

The writer to be considered next is difficult to date. Estimates range from the beginning of the second century, if not the end of the first, on to the middle of that century. Perhaps we cannot do better than accept the date given by Williston Walker in his classic *A History of the Christian Church* and place the writing of Hermas as falling somewhere between 115 and 140.

Hermas appears to have been of the church at Rome, and one of those leaders known in the early church as prophets. When Paul says in I Cor. 12: 28, "And God has appointed in the church first

apostles, second prophets, third teachers," the main
distinction appears to be that the apostles gave the
Christian message to unbelievers, while the prophets spoke to those already in the churches, and the
teachers explained or interpreted Christian truth.
However, the distinction is blurred at the edges. In
I Cor. 14:3-5 the contribution of the prophet, ex-
ceeding that of one who speaks in tongues, is the
upbuilding, encouragement, and consolation of the
church, while in Acts 21:10-11 the prophet is the
spokesman of the Holy Spirit, thereby predicting
the future.

The second-century church apparently regarded
Hermas as a prophet in both senses, for the most
certain fact we know about him is that his long
piece of writing, commonly known as the Shepherd
of Hermas, was circulated among the churches and
for a considerable time was in and out of the New
Testament canon. It was accepted as scripture by
Irenaeus and by Clement of Alexandria toward the
end of the second century and by Origen in the
third. However, Eusebius rejected it, as does the
Muratorian canon, which lists the books in use in
the church at Rome about the end of the second
century. With this list stands the interesting obser-
vation, "The Shepherd of Hermas may be read but
not publicly in church."

The church was doubtless wise in its exclusion.
The book is not only long but verbose, and in
spiritual range and depth it appears inferior to the
other writings presented thus far. It is in three

65

parts: the Visions, in the last of which the shepherd appears as the angel of repentance; the Mandates, or commandments; and the Similitudes, or parables. The general tone is apocalyptic, and it was probably regarded by the early church as a supplement to the book of Revelation. This may account for its long acceptance as scripture.

Whatever the shortcomings of the book, the writer has an important point which he reiterates again and again. In fact, it is a two-sided point. On the one hand, the author stresses the Christian requirements of good moral living in obedience to God and points to the temptations which are rampant in the world and seek entrance into the church. The other side of his message is the need and the possibility of divine acceptance through repentance. By the time Hermas wrote, many had come to believe that there was no hope of salvation for the Christian who had sinned after baptism, as many obviously had. Hermas was more charitable, and believed God to be. He is usually interpreted as saying that there could be a second chance, but none beyond this point. As I read him, I do not find this limitation nearly so prominent as his stress on the fact that the sinner who repents need not abandon hope.

Hermas' visions and parables are pointed and often interesting, but they do not glow with the marks of genius. Though explained point for point, they often seem too labored. Yet if one may judge from his writing, Hermas was a man of some literary talent who wished to use it wholly for the Lord. If one may substitute preacher for prophet in Paul's word to the Corinthian church, Hermas was in a sense a prototype of the preacher of today who "speaks to men for their upbuilding and encouragement and consolation" (I Cor. 14:3). And this is no small achievement, whether in the second century or the twentieth.

1. *Living Stones*

A large part of the first section of the Shepherd consists of visions shown to Hermas by an old woman, who is the church from the beginning of creation, and she shows him the church of his time in the form of a tower in the process of formation. As he queries regarding the stones which go into it and those which are unacceptable, she interprets each kind. Beneath the symbolism it is apparent that human nature in the second century was much like that of the present.

"Now hear about the stones that go into the building. The stones that are square and white and fit their joints are the apostles and bishops and teachers and deacons who have lived in the holiness of God, and have been bishops and teachers and deacons for God's chosen in purity and reverence. Some of them have fallen asleep, and others are still living. They always agreed with one another and were at peace with one another, and listened to one another; that is why their joints fit together in the building of the tower."

"But the ones that are dragged out of the deep, and put into the building, and that agree in their joints with the other stones already laid, who are they?"

"They are those who have suffered for the name of the Lord."

"But I want to know who the other stones are, that are brought from the dry land, my lady."

"Those that go into the building without being shaped, the Lord has approved, because they lived in the uprightness of the Lord, and carried out his commands."

"But who are the ones that are brought and set in the building?"

"They are young in the faith, and faithful, but they are exhorted by the angels to do right, because wickedness has been found in them."

"But who are the ones that they were rejecting and throwing away?"

"They are the ones that have sinned and want to repent. That is why they were not thrown far from the tower, because they will be of use in the building if they repent. So those who are going to repent will be strong in the faith, if they repent now, while the tower is being built, but if the building is finished, they will no longer have an opportunity, but will be outcasts. The only thing they have is that they lie near the tower.

"But do you want to know who they are that were broken up and thrown far away from the tower? They are the sons of disobedience; their faith was hypocritical, and no wickedness escaped them. That is why they have no salvation, for on account of their wickedness they are of no use in building. That is why they were broken in pieces and thrown far away, because of the Lord's anger, for they angered him. And as to the others that you saw lying about in such numbers, and not going into the building, the scaly ones are the ones that have learned the truth, but do not stand by it."

"But who are the ones that were cracked?"

"They are those who are against one another in their hearts and are not at peace with one another, but keep up an appearance of peace, but when they leave one another, their wicked thoughts remain in their hearts. These are the cracks that the stones have. But the ones that are too short are those who have believed and live for the most part in uprightness, but they have some fraction of disobedience; that is why they are too short and not perfect."

"But the white and rounded ones, that would not fit into the building, who are they, my lady?"

She answered, and said to me,

"How long are you going to be foolish and stupid, and ask about everything and perceive nothing? They are those who have faith, but have also the riches of this world. When persecution comes, because of their riches and their business affairs they deny their Lord." I answered her and said,

"My lady, when then will they be of use for the building?"

"When," she said, "their riches, which lead their souls astray, shall be cut off, then they will be useful to God. For just as the round stone cannot be made square unless it is cut off and loses some part of itself, so those also who have this world's riches cannot be of use to the Lord unless their riches are cut off. Learn first from your own case; when you were rich, you were useless, but now you are useful and beneficial to life. Be useful to God, for you yourself also benefit from the same stones."

COMPARE I PET. 2:1-10.

2. *Stong Foundations*

The Shepherd of Hermas has been called the *Pilgrim's Progress* of the early church. While this is not its style throughout, an illustration of its Bunyan-like flavor is its description of seven virtues that support the tower which is the church.

Then when I had stopped asking her about all these things, she said to me,

"Would you like to see something else?"

As I was very eager to see more, I was delighted that I was to do so. She looked at me with a smile and said to me,

"Do you see seven women around the tower?"

"Yes, my lady," said I.

"This tower is supported by them, by the Lord's

command. Now listen to their activities. The first of them, who is clasping her hands, is called Faith; through her God's chosen are saved. The next one, who is dressed for work and acts like a man, is called Self-control; she is the daughter of Faith. Whoever follows her will have a happy life, because he will refrain from all evil-doing, believing that if he refrains from every evil passion he will make sure of eternal life."

"And who are the others, my lady?"

"They are daughters one of another, and they are named one of them Sincerity, and the next Knowledge, and the next Innocence, and the next Reverence, and the next Love. So when you do all the deeds of their mother, you can attain life."

"I would like to know, my lady," said I, "what power each of them possesses."

"Listen," she said, "to the powers that they possess. Their powers are controlled by one another, and they follow one another, in the order in which they were born. From Faith springs Self-control, from Self-control, Sincerity, from Sincerity, Innocence, from Innocence, Reverence, from Reverence, Knowledge, from Knowledge, Love. So their deeds are pure, reverent, and divine. So whoever serves these, and has the strength to master their deeds, will have his home in the tower, with the saints of God.

COMPARE II PET. 1:3-11.

3. *The Working of Ill Temper*

In the Mandates, the shepherd, who appears to Hermas as the angel of repentance, gives counsel on various temptations that assail the Christian. These words on ill temper are expressed in the diction of the primitive church but describe accurately the occasions and effects of ill temper in any period.

"Hear, then," said he, "the working of ill temper, and how evil it is and how it destroys the servants of God by its working, and how it leads them astray from righteousness. But it does not lead astray those who are filled with faith, nor can it work evil to them, because my power is with them, but it leads astray those who are vain and double-minded. And when it sees such men in tranquillity, it forces its way into the heart of that man, and the man or woman is made bitter out of nothing, because of daily business or of food or some trifle, or about some friend, or about giving or receiving, or about some such foolish matters. For all these things are foolish and vain and meaningless, and unprofitable to the servants of God. But long-suffering is great and mighty and has steadfast power and prospers in great breadth, is joyful, glad, without care, glorifying the Lord at every time, has nothing bitter in itself, but remains ever meek and gentle. Therefore this long-suffering dwells with those who have faith in perfectness.

"But ill temper is first foolish, frivolous, and silly; then from silliness comes bitterness, from bitterness wrath, from wrath rage, and from rage fury; then fury, being compounded of such great evils, becomes great and inexpiable sin. For when these spirits dwell in one vessel, where also the Holy Spirit dwells, there is not room in that vessel, but it is over-crowded. Therefore the delicate spirit which is unaccustomed to dwell with an evil spirit, or with hardness, departs from such a man, and seeks to dwell with gentleness and quietness. Then, when it departs from that man where it was dwelling, that man becomes empty of the righteous spirit, and for the future is filled with the evil spirits, and is disorderly in all his actions, being dragged here and there by the evil spirits, and is wholly blinded from goodness of thought. Thus, then, it happens with all who are ill tempered.

"Abstain then from ill temper, that most evil spirit, but put on long-suffering and withstand ill temper, and be found with the holiness which is beloved of the Lord. See then that you forget not this commandment, for if you master this commandment you will also be able to keep the other commandments which I am going to give you. Be strong in them and strengthen yourself, and let all strengthen themselves who wish to walk in them." [1]

COMPARE JAMES 3.

[1] Since Lake places an entire chapter in one paragraph and this is an unusually long one, I have broken it up into shorter paragraphs. This is done in the next two excerpts not only for this reason but because of the conversational nature of the material.

4. *To Live to God*

The angel of repentance enumerates to Hermas a long list of evil acts and attitudes from which the Christian is enjoined to refrain. Yet his approach is not wholly negative. Asked to say what deeds are right, he replies with a corresponding list of what will enable the Christian to live to God.

"And explain to me, sir," said I, "the power of the things which are good, that I may walk in them and serve them, that by doing them I may be saved."

"Listen, then," said he, "to the deeds of goodness, which you must do and not refrain from them. First of all, faith, fear of God, love and harmony, words of righteousness, truth, patience; than these there is nothing better in the life of man. If any man keep these things and do not refrain from them, he becomes blessed in his life. Next hear the things which follow: To minister to widows, to look after orphans and the destitute, to redeem from distress the servants of God, to be hospitable, for in hospitality may be found the practice of good, to resist none, to be gentle, to be poorer than all men, to reverence the aged, to practise justice, to preserve brotherhood, to submit to insult, to be brave, to bear no malice, to comfort those who are oppressed in spirit, not to cast aside those who are offended in the faith, but to convert them and give them courage, to reprove sinners, not to oppress poor debtors, and whatever is like to these things. Do you not think," said he, "that these things are good?"

"Yes, sir," said I, "for what is better than these things?"

"Walk then," said he, "in them, and do not refrain from them, and you shall live to God. Keep therefore this commandment. If you do good, and do not refrain from it, you shall live to God, and all who act so shall live to God. And again, if you do not do that which is wicked, and refrain from it, you shall live to God, and all shall live to God who keep these commandments and walk in them."

COMPARE JAS. 1:16-27.

5. *The Sum of the Matter*

A common theme in the Similitudes is the differences among Christians, who vary according to their obedience and responsiveness to God. For example, sticks cut from the same willow tree and returned to the angel of the Lord differ greatly when given back, but even though they have become dry, there is a chance for healthy growth when they are planted and watered. Twelve mountains represent as many kinds of believers. The figure of the stones used in building the tower reappears, some being acceptable while others must be rejected.

Since the parables are long, each requiring usually several chapters for presentation and interpretation, it would not be profitable to try to reproduce them here. The final exhortation of the shepherd, summing up the call to repentance in briefer similes, is as follows.

75

"Therefore, amend yourselves while the tower is still being built. The Lord dwells among men who love peace, for of a truth peace is dear to him, but he is far away from the contentious and those who are destroyed by malice. Give back then to him your spirit whole as you received it. For if you give to the dyer a new garment whole, and wish to receive it back from him whole, but the dyer gives it back to you torn, will you accept it? Will you not at once grow hot and pursue him with abuse, saying 'I gave you a whole garment, why have you torn it and given it back to me useless? And because of the tear which you have made in it it cannot be used.' Will you not say all these things to the dyer about the rent which he has made in your garment? If then you are grieved with your garment, and complain that you did not receive it back whole, what do you think the Lord will do to you, who gave you the spirit whole, and you have returned it altogether useless, so that it can be of no use to its Lord, for its use began to be useless when it had been corrupted by you. Will not therefore the Lord of that spirit punish you with death, because of this deed of yours?"

"Certainly," said I, "He will punish all those whom he finds keeping the memory of offences."

"Do not then," said he, "trample on his mercy, but rather honour him that he is so patient to your offences and is not as you are. Repent therefore with the repentance that avails you.

"All these things which have been written above

76

I, the shepherd, the angel of repentance, have declared and spoken to the servants of God. If then you shall believe and shall listen to my words and shall walk in them, and shall correct your ways, you shall be able to live. But if you shall remain in malice and in the memory of offences, none of such kind shall live to God. All these things that I must tell have been told to you."

The shepherd himself said to me, "Have you asked me about everything?" And I said: "Yes, Sir."

"Why then did you not ask me about the marks of the stones which were placed in the building, why we filled up the marks?" And I said, "I forgot, Sir."

"Listen now," said he, "about them. These are those who heard my commandments, and repented with all their hearts. And when the Lord saw that their repentance was good and pure, and that they could remain in it, he commanded their former sins to be blotted out. For these marks were their sins, and they were made level that they should not appear."

COMPARE I JOHN 1:5–2:6.

The Letter of Barnabas

We come now to a writing of the early church which, like First Clement and the Shepherd of Hermas, was in and out of the New Testament canon for a considerable period. Accepted as scripture by both Clement of Alexandria and Origen, it stands directly after the Revelation of St. John in the Codex Sinaiticus, which the German scholar Tischendorf found in the monastery of St. Catherine on Mt. Sinai in 1859 and dramatically preserved to posterity.[1] This indicates that it was still

[1] While visiting the monastery in 1844, Tischendorf discovered by accident forty-three leaves of a New Testa-

being regarded as scripture as late as the middle of the fourth century.

We do not know who wrote it. Though the assumption that its author was Barnabas the companion of Paul doubtless helped to give it biblical status, its mood and setting are very different from those of what Barnabas would have written. It was either written by some other person of that name or, more likely as was common in that period, by some earnest but anonymous Christian who hoped to gain a hearing by using a familiar and respected pseudonym.

Neither is it possible to date it with accuracy, or to know to what group the letter was addressed. The date generally ascribed to it is about 130, chiefly on the basis of a reference in chapter 16 to a temple built in Jerusalem by a heathen, which may

---

ment manuscript in a scrap basket. These were given to him to take home. No more could then be found, but believing that more must be there, he returned in 1853 but was without success. He returned again in 1859 under the patronage of the Czar of Russia. On the evening before his departure a steward took him to his cell and showed Tischendorf the manuscript he had so long sought. Finding that it contained the entire Greek text of the Letter of Barnabas, which had not previously been known to exist in Greek, he sat up all night to copy it.

The manuscript, since then known as the Codex Sinaiticus, was presented to the Czar of Russia and placed in the imperial library at St. Petersburg, now Leningrad. In 1934 the Soviet Government sold the manuscript to the British Museum, where it now resides. While not the earliest codex, it is the only uncial Greek manuscript that contains the whole New Testament and therefore is of immense value to textual scholarship.

refer to Hadrian's temple to Jupiter erected in 130/31. However, some date it much earlier, at the end of the first century, and perhaps even prior to First Clement.

From its content the letter appears to have been written by a Gentile Christian teacher, perhaps at Alexandria and certainly in the Alexandrian school of thought, who was eager to preserve the Old Testament to the Christian faith without taking literally the Judaic law. Not only did he wish to preserve the validity of the Old Testament, which Marcion and some of the Gnostics were rejecting, but he desired to fix attention on the demands of moral living required of the Christian—"the new law of our Lord Jesus Christ," as he calls it—as over against both the requirements of the Jewish law and the antinomianism which could be deduced from salvation by faith alone. The latter objective, as has doubtless been noted from earlier selections, was a note frequently sounded by the Christian writers of this period.

Both these purposes were valid ones. And in both, Barnabas—for so we shall call him for lack of a better name—made significant contributions. Yet not without serious limitations. His treatment of the Old Testament is primarily allegorical. Passage after passage is quoted, quite largely from the Law, the Prophets, and Psalms, and the author professes to give the Christian meaning foreshadowed by the passage. As one reads his comments on these great, familiar passages, it is difficult to escape the feeling that Barnabas might better have let them speak for themselves! The conclusions he draws seem usually to be true enough but often far-fetched. It is an example of what in homiletics is called eisegesis in contrast with exegesis, which aims to discover and present the original meaning of a passage of scripture.

Much the same judgment may be passed on the author's treatment of the moral imperatives of the Christian in obedience to the will of God. He has many true insights, but they are at times encased in legalistic injunctions and prohibitions. The Greek version of the manuscript includes at the end, while the Latin does not, the "two ways" of light and darkness which are also embodied in the Didache, at which we will look presently. Here are incorporated brief commands, twenty-three of them positive and twenty-eight negative, which Christians for the most part still recognize as injunctions of Christian morality.

In the selections which follow these tendencies both in their points of strength and of weakness will be evident. The church did well in the winnowing processes of time to omit the letter from the biblical canon, for it does not glow with the serene wisdom of Clement or the fiery faith of Ignatius. Yet any shortcomings should not cancel out the real value of the writing, which served a useful purpose in its time and is strewn with observations still applicable to life today.

1. *Let Knowledge Be Perfected Along with Faith*

While the salutation with which this letter opens does not tell us to whom the author is writing, it does tell us much about them. These sons and daughters in the Lord were Christians whose lives so manifested the gift of the Spirit that because of them Barnabas felt more assured of his own salvation. Apparently after having visited them he felt such a lift in his own spirit that he felt impelled to write them of some of the things he felt the Lord had taught him. Were this pastor-and-people or teacher-and-taught relationship more common today, we should hear less about this being a post-Christian era.

Hail, sons and daughters, in the name of the Lord who loved us, in peace.

Exceedingly and abundantly do I rejoice over your blessed and glorious spirit for the greatness and richness of God's ordinances towards you; so innate a grace of the gift of the spirit have you received. Wherefore I congratulate myself the more in my hope of salvation, because I truly see in you that the Spirit has been poured out upon you from the Lord, who is rich in his bounty; so that the sight of you, for which I longed, amazed me. Being persuaded then of this, and being conscious that since I spoke among you I have much understanding because the Lord has traveled with me in the way of righteousness, I am above all constrained to this, to love you above my own life, because great faith and love dwell in you in the hope of his life. I have therefore reckoned that, if I make it my care in your behalf to communicate somewhat of that which I received, it shall bring me the reward of having ministered to such spirits, and I hasten to send you a short letter in order that your knowledge may be perfected along with your faith.

There are then three doctrines of the Lord: the hope of life is the beginning and end of our faith; and righteousness is the beginning and end of judgment; love of joy and of gladness is the testimony of the works of righteousness. For the Lord made known to us through the prophets things past and things present and has given us the first fruits of the taste of things to come; and when we see these things coming to pass one by one, as he said, we ought to make a richer and deeper offering for fear of him. But I will show you a few things, not as a teacher but as one of yourselves, in which you shall rejoice at this present time.

COMPARE I COR. 1:1-9.

2. *Counsel for Evil Days*

In this passage is illustrated the author's use of the Old Testament in a mood which is quite congenial to modern thought. While the challenging of great political and economic structures was not the concern of the early church—as a tiny minority they could have accomplished little if they had attempted it—the motives to social action which must actuate us in our effort were very much in their thinking.

Seeing then that the days are evil, and that the worker of evil himself is in power, we ought to give heed to ourselves, and seek out the ordinances of the Lord. Fear, then, and patience are the helpers of our faith, and long-suffering and continence are our allies. While then these things remain in holiness towards the Lord, wisdom, prudence, understanding, and knowledge rejoice with them. For he has made plain to us through all the prophets that he needs neither sacrifices nor burnt-offerings nor oblations, saying in one place, "What is the multitude of your sacrifices unto me? saith the Lord. I am full of burnt offerings and desire not the fat of lambs and the blood of bulls and goats, not even when ye come to appear before me. For who has required these things at your hands? Henceforth shall ye tread my court no more. If ye bring flour, it is vain. Incense is an abomination to me. I cannot away with your new moons and sabbaths."

These things then he abolished in order that the new law of our Lord Jesus Christ, which is without the yoke of necessity, might have its oblation not made by man. And again he says to them, "Did I command your fathers when they came out of the land of Egypt to offer me burnt offerings and sacrifices? Nay, but rather did I command them this: Let none of you cherish any evil in his heart against his neighbour, and love not a false oath." We ought then to understand, if we are not foolish, the loving intention of our Father, for he speaks to us, wishing that we should not err like them, but seek how we may make our offering to him. To us then he speaks thus: "Sacrifice for the Lord is a broken heart, a smell of sweet savour to the Lord is a heart that glorifieth him that made it." [2] We ought, therefore, brethren, carefully to enquire concerning our salvation, in order that the evil one may not achieve a deceitful entry into us and hurl us away from our life.

COMPARE ISA. 1:10-17.

3. *Of True Fasting*

This passage, which directly follows the preceding in the text, is in a similar vein but is much more explicit as to the moral obligations of the Christian toward his neighbor, and especially toward his hungry and suffering neighbor.

So he says to them again about this, "Why do you fast to me, says the Lord, so that your voice is

[2] Lake in his translation, which has been used in this excerpt, comments on this quotation, "The first part of this quotation is Ps. 51:17; the second part according to a note in C [Codex Constantinopolitanus] is from the Apocalypse of Adam, which is no longer extant." Since Lake has used the diction of the King James Version in rendering the author's quotations, it might be well to read Isa. 1:10-17 in this version also. The archaic phrase "I cannot away with" appears in the Revised Standard Version as "I cannot endure."

85

raised in a cry to me? This is not the fast that I have chosen, says the Lord, not a man humbling his soul, not even if you bend your neck like a ring, and put on sackcloth and lie in ashes, not even so can you call it an acceptable fast." But to you he says, "Behold, this is the fast I have chosen, says the Lord: Undo every unrighteous bond, untie the knots of violent agreements, set the bruised at liberty, and tear up every unfair contract. Break your bread to the hungry, and if you see a man naked, clothe him. Take the homeless into your house, and if you see a humble person, you shall not look down on him, nor shall the members of your household. Then your light will break forth early in the morning and your healing will rise quickly, and your uprightness will go before you and the glory of the Lord will envelop you. Then you will cry out and God will hear you; while you are still speaking, he will say, Here I am! if you strip from you every fetter and lifting up of the hand, and grumbling word, and give your bread to the hungry from your heart, and show pity to the soul that is oppressed." So, brethren, he that is long suffering, foreseeing that the people he had prepared in his Beloved would believe in guilelessness, made all plain to us beforehand, so that we might not suffer shipwreck by being converted to their law.

Compare Isa. 58:1-10.

4. *Eat No Unclean Thing*

The following is a good example of the way in which Barnabas often takes Old Testament passages, such as the dietary injunctions found in the fourteenth chapter of Deuteronomy, and on the assumption that "Moses spoke in the spirit" draws from them moral deductions for Christian behavior. Though it may be doubted that Moses meant by these forbidden foods all that Barnabas makes him mean, what results from this eisegesis is a vivid picture of human frailties.

Now, because Moses said, "You shall not eat swine or eagle or hawk or crow or any fish that does not have scales on it," he had three teachings in mind. Further, he says to them in Deuteronomy, "And I will set forth my ordinances to this people." So, then, God's command is not that they should not eat, but Moses spoke in the spirit. This, then, is why he mentioned the swine: "You shall not associate," he means, "with men who are like swine," that is, when they are in luxury, they forget the Lord, but when they are in want they acknowledge the Lord, just as the swine when it is feeding does not know its master, but when it is hungry it squeals, and when it has been fed, it is quiet again. "Neither shall you eat the eagle or the hawk or the kite or the crow"; you shall not, he means, associate with or come to resemble such men as do not know how to provide their food by toil and sweat, but lawlessly seize what belongs to others, and while pretending to live in innocence, watch and look

87

about to find whom they can plunder in their greed, just as these birds are the only ones that provide no food for themselves, but sit idle and seek ways to eat the meat of others, since they are pests in wickedness. "And you shall not eat," he goes on, "sea eel or polyp or cuttlefish," You shall not, he means, associate with such men and come to resemble them, who are utterly ungodly and already condemned to death, just as these fish alone are accursed and swim in the depths, not swimming on the surface like the rest, but living in the mud on the bottom. . . . Moses received three decrees about food and uttered them in the spirit, but they in their fleshly desire received them as having to do with eating. But David understands the meaning of these three decrees, and says, "Blessed is the man who has not gone in the counsel of the ungodly"— as the fish go in darkness to the bottom; "and has not stood in the pathway of sinners"—as those who claim to fear the Lord but sin like the swine; "and has not sat in the seat of the pestilent," like birds that sit and wait for their prey. You have in full the lesson about eating.

COMPARE DEUT. 14:3-20; MARK 7:14-23.

5. *A Temple of the Lord*

The author's presentation of the Christian's living and speaking as a temple being built for and by the Lord suggests Paul's metaphor of the body as the

88

temple of the Holy Spirit, but the setting is quite different. Though the quotation which introduces it appears to be garbled, the passage is one of the finest in the letter.

But let us inquire if a temple of God exists. Yes, it exists, where he himself said that he makes and perfects it. For it is written, "And it shall come to pass when the week is ended that a temple of God shall be built gloriously in the name of the Lord." I find then that a temple exists. Learn then how it will be built in the name of the Lord. Before we believed in God the habitation of our heart was corrupt and weak, like a temple really built with hands, because it was full of idolatry, and was the house of demons through doing things which were contrary to God. "But it shall be built in the name of the Lord." Now give heed, in order that the temple of the Lord may be built gloriously. Learn in what way. When we received the remission of sins, and put our hope on the Name, we became new, being created again from the beginning; wherefore God truly dwells in us, in the habitation which we are. How? His word of faith, the calling of his promise, the wisdom of the ordinances, the commands of the teaching, himself prophesying in us, himself dwelling in us, by opening the door of the temple (that is the mouth) to us, giving repentance to us, and thus he leads us, who have been enslaved to death, into the incorruptible temple. For he who desires to be saved looks not at the man, but at him

89

who dwells and speaks in him, and is amazed at him, for he has never either heard him speak such words with his mouth, nor has he himself ever desired to hear them. This is a spiritual temple being built for the Lord.

COMPARE I COR. 3:16-17; 6:19-20.

The Didache

The Didache, otherwise known as the Teaching of the Twelve Apostles, was formerly believed to be a very early document, perhaps antedating First Clement. While most of the scholars concerned with this period have now revised this estimate, there is no complete agreement as to its date or literary history. The issue is complicated by the fact that it contains two quite different parts, rather lamely joined together, which quite probably were separate documents amalgamated at some time during the first half of the second century by some unknown editor.

The first of these components, as has been indicated in the previous section, is "the way of life and death," often referred to as "the two ways"; this appears both at the end of the letter of Barnabas and at the beginning of the Didache. The forms are not identical, for that in the Didache incorporates various sayings of Jesus from Matthew and Luke, these being primarily from the Sermon on the Mount. In the letter of Barnabas they are called the ways of light and darkness. Yet the similarity is unmistakable.

Scholars are about equally divided in their opinions as to which was written first, and there is considerable likelihood that both are adaptations from an earlier document. There is extant in Latin, though not in Greek, a briefer and perhaps earlier form of the "two ways," but whether this is an accurate translation of the original is still an unanswered question.

The second section of the Didache is a manual of church order, very important from a historical standpoint as giving a picture of the church of its times. It gives instructions with regard to baptism, the Lord's Supper, fasting, prayer and the use of the Lord's Prayer, the treatment of visiting teachers and so-called prophets, worship on the Lord's Day, and the appointment of bishops and deacons. In conjunction with the instructions for the *agape* meal there are two beautiful eucharistic prayers.

What period does this reflect? While the problem of date and authorship of the Didache as a whole and of both its components is by no means solved, it seems probable that this manual of church order does give a true picture of conditions in the church around the end of the first century. In any case, the Lord's Supper appears still to have been a real supper, a communal meal; there were bishops (overseers) and deacons for each church, and the authority was not yet vested in a single bishop presiding over a considerable territory; the gift of prophecy was still being exercised, though with perversions against which warnings are included. These traveling prophets, or missionaries, claimed to speak in the Spirit but apparently, then as now, there was a doubt about it, and there is sound wisdom in the words, "But not everyone who speaks in ecstatic utterances is a prophet, but only if he behaves in the ways of the Lord." (11:8).

To sum up, the Didache dates from the second century and could have been compiled by an editor as late as A.D. 150, but its two sources are apparently much earlier and possibly as early as the end of the first century. The editor apparently intended to present the two ways, of life and death, as a set of injunctions for catechumens preparatory to baptism; but the arrangement is artificial, for such a moral catechism lacks the note of saving faith so central to early Christianity. Nevertheless, the compilation contains for the most part not only sound moral wisdom but a vivid picture of daily life and Chris-

tian worship in the early church. We must be deeply grateful that both components, and particularly
the second, have been preserved.

1. *The Way of Life*

Did the author of the Didache or of the Letter of
Barnabas originate "the two ways" of life and death?
If one copied from the other, which did the copying?
Or did both make adaptations from a common source?
This is an unanswered literary question. But since
they are most familiar as an introduction to the Didache and since the two sides of the injunctions should
be looked at together, we include both in this compilation of early teaching as to the good life.

There are two ways, one of life and one of death,
and there is a great difference between the two
ways.

The way of life is this: first, you shall love God,
who made you; second, your neighbor as yourself;
and everything that you would not have done to
you, do not do to another.

Now the teaching of these words is this: Bless
those that curse you, and pray for your enemies,
and fast for those that persecute you; for what merit
is there if you love those that love you? Do not
even the heathen do that? But love those that hate
you, and you will have no enemy.

Abstain from physical and bodily cravings. If

94

someone strikes you on the right cheek, turn the other to him too, and you will be perfect. If anyone forces you to go one mile, go two miles with him. If anyone takes away your coat, give him your shirt too. If anyone takes from you what is yours, do not demand it back, for you cannot.

Give to everyone that asks of you, and do not demand it back. For the Father wishes that from his own gifts it should be given to all. Blessed is he who gives according to the command, for he is innocent. Woe to him who receives; for if a man receives because he is in need, he will be innocent; but he who receives when he is not in need will stand trial, as to why he received and for what, and being put in prison he will be examined about what he has done, and he will not come out of it until he pays the last penny. But of this it was also said, "Let your charity sweat in your hands until you know to whom to give."

The second commandment of the Teaching is: You shall not murder, you shall not commit adultery, you shall not corrupt boys, you shall not commit fornication, you shall not steal, you shall not practice magic, you shall not use enchantments, you shall not murder a child by abortion, or kill one when it is born. You shall not desire your neighbor's goods, you shall not commit perjury, you shall not bear false witness, you shall not speak evil, you shall not hold a grudge. You shall not be double-minded, nor double-tongued, for the double tongue is a deadly snare. Your speech shall not be false or vain, but fulfilled in action. You shall not be covetous or rapacious, or a hypocrite or malicious or proud. You shall not entertain an evil design against your neighbor. You shall not hate any man, but some you shall reprove, and for some you shall pray, and some you shall love more than your life.

My child, flee from everyone evil, and from everyone like him. Do not be irascible, for anger leads to murder, or jealous, or contentious or passionate; for all these things breed murders.

My child, do not be lustful, for lust leads to fornication, or foul-spoken or one who lifts up his eyes; for all these things breed adulteries.

My child, do not be a dealer in omens, since it leads to idolatry, or an enchanter, or an astrologer, or a magician, and do not wish to see or hear them, for all these things breed idolatry.

My child, do not be a liar, since lying leads to theft, or avaricious, or vainglorious, for all these things breed thefts.

My child, do not be a grumbler, since it leads to blasphemy, or self-willed or evil-minded, for all these things breed blasphemies; but be meek, since the meek will inherit the earth. Be long-suffering and merciful and guileless, and quiet and good, and always revere the words that you have heard. You shall not exalt yourself, or admit arrogance to your soul. Your soul shall not associate with lofty men, but you shall live with upright and humble men.

You shall accept the experiences that befall you as good, knowing that nothing happens without God.

My child, night and day you shall remember him who speaks the word of God to you, and you shall honor him as the Lord, for where the Lord's nature is talked of, there the Lord is. And you shall seek daily the faces of the saints, to find rest in their words. You shall not cause division, but you shall reconcile fighters. You shall judge uprightly, and you shall not show partiality in reproving transgressions. You shall not doubt whether it will be or not.

Do not be stretching out your hands to take, and closing them when it comes to giving. If you have earned it through your hands, you shall give a ransom for your sins. You shall not hesitate to give, nor grumble when you give, for you shall know who is the good payer of wages. You shall not turn the needy away, but you shall share everything with your brother, and you shall not say it is your own. For if you share in what is immortal, how much more in mortal things!

You shall not withhold your hand from your son or from your daughter, but from their youth up you shall teach them the fear of God. You shall not give orders in bitterness to your man or woman slave, who hope in the same God, lest they cease to fear the God who is over you both; for he came not to call men with partiality, but those whom the Spirit prepared. And you slaves shall obey your masters, as a symbol of God, with modesty and fear. You shall hate all hypocrisy, and everything that is not pleasing to the Lord.

You must not forsake the commandments of the Lord, but you shall keep the teachings you have received, neither adding to them nor taking from them. In church you shall confess your transgressions, and you shall not approach prayer with an evil conscience. This is the way of life.

COMPARE ROMANS 12.

2. *The Way of Death*

Here is a catalog of "the sin which doth so easily beset us." Granted, it is not pleasant reading. But neither are the procedures it enumerates beautiful! Furthermore, it is a sobering thought that with few exceptions this is a picture of the temptations that beset the unwary, even Christians, in the life of today.

But the way of death is this: First of all, it is wicked and full of cursing; murders, adulteries, lusts, fornications, thefts, idolatries, magic arts, enchantments, robberies, false witnessings, hypocrisies, duplicity, fraud, pride, malice, willfulness, covetousness, foul speech, jealousy, arrogance, exaltation, boastfulness. Persecutors of good men, hating truth, loving falsehood, ignorant of the wages of uprightness, not adhering to what is good, nor to upright judgment, lying awake not for what is good but for what is evil, from whom gentleness and patience are far away, loving vanity, seeking reward, without pity for the poor, not toiling for the oppressed, ignoring their Maker, murderers of children, corrupters of God's creatures, turning away the needy, oppressing the afflicted, advocates of the rich, unjust judges of the poor, utterly sinful. May you be delivered, my children, from all these!

See that no one leads you astray from this way of the Teaching, for he teaches you without God. For if you can bear the whole yoke of the Lord, you will be perfect; but if you cannot, do what you can.

COMPARE ROM. 1:28-32; GAL. 5:19-24.

3. *Two Eucharistic Prayers*

These eucharistic prayers, so expressive of deep devotion, are modeled in form after the Jewish forms of grace before and after meals, yet with a distinctly Christian note. The reference to the gathering of the church together from the ends of the earth into the kingdom of God has made the passage a familiar one in this ecumenical age.

Now about the Thanksgiving, give thanks thus: First about the cup, "We thank you, our Father, for the holy vine of your servant David, which you have made known to us through your servant Jesus. Glory to you forever." And about the piece of bread,

"We thank you, our Father, for the life and knowledge you have made known to us through Jesus your servant. Glory be yours forever. Just as this piece of bread was scattered over the mountains, and then was gathered together and became one, so let your church be gathered together from the ends of the earth into your kingdom. For the glory and the power are yours through Jesus Christ forever." . . .

After you are satisfied, give thanks thus: "We give you thanks, Holy Father, for your holy name, which you have made dwell in our hearts, and for knowledge and faith and immortality, which you have made known to us through Jesus your servant; glory to you forever. You, almighty Master, have created all things for your name's sake, you have given men food and drink to enjoy, that they may give you thanks, but you have granted us spiritual food and drink and everlasting life through your servant. Above all we thank you that you are mighty; glory to you forever. Remember, Lord, your church, to save it from all evil and to make it perfect in your love, and gather it together in its holiness from the four winds, into your kingdom which you have prepared for it. For the power and the glory are yours forever. Let your favor come and this world pass away. Hosanna to the God of David! If anyone is holy, let him come; if anyone is not, let him repent. Lord, come quickly! Amen." But permit the prophets to give thanks as much as they please.

COMPARE I CHRON. 29:10-13; JOHN 17:20-26.

4. *For Peace and Purity*

The three paragraphs which follow deal with different themes—themes of major importance to the church then and the church now. Yet they are bound together by the common thread of fidelity to the gospel as Christians are urged to "maintain the unity of the Spirit in the bond of peace."

On every Lord's Day—his special day—come together and break bread and give thanks, first confessing your sins so that your sacrifice may be pure. Anyone at variance with his neighbor must not join you, until they are reconciled, lest your sacrifice be defiled. For it was of this sacrifice that the Lord said, "Always and everywhere offer me a pure sacrifice; for I am a great King, says the Lord, and my name is marveled at by the nations."

You must, then, elect for yourselves bishops and deacons who are a credit to the Lord, men who are gentle, generous, faithful and well tried. For their ministry to you is identical with that of the prophets and teachers. You must not, therefore, despise them, for along with the prophets and teachers they enjoy a place of honor among you.

Furthermore, do not reprove each other angrily,

101

but quietly, as you find it in the gospel. Moreover, if anyone has wronged his neighbor, nobody must speak to him, and he must not hear a word from you, until he repents. Say your prayers, give your charity, and do everything just as you find it in the gospel of our Lord.

COMPARE EPH. 4:1-7, 11-16.

Second Clement

The writing we are about to consider has traditionally been regarded as a second letter of Clement
the Bishop of Rome to the church at Corinth, and
in many collections of the writings from the early
church it stands directly after the document with
which this anthology begins. If this were its authorship, it would date from the end of the first century
or the earliest years of the second. While we do not
know who did write it, it is virtually certain that
Clement of Rome did not, and it is much more likely to have been written at Alexandria than Rome.

Its content fits more aptly the middle of the second century than anything much earlier than that.

In fact, it is not a letter at all but a Christian sermon—the earliest preserved with the exception of the book of James in the New Testament. Its purpose appears to be to combat Gnostic heresies and at the same time to give good moral counsel to the Christians to whom it is addressed. As over against the Gnostic idea that Christ was something more than man but less than God, the highest of the emanations from God, the author stresses the full divinity of Christ. In contrast with the Gnostic view that the body is essentially evil, he views it as good if it is kept pure as God intends it to be, and he makes much of the resurrection of the flesh. A third major note is his conception of the church as a preexistent spiritual reality which took visible form in the flesh of Christ and continues in the flesh of the Christian as long as the flesh is maintained in purity, thus becoming an extension of the incarnation. This last point, though it bears some resemblance to Paul's imagery of the church as the body of Christ, rests on a very different conception, a Platonic conception of the phenomenal world as a copy of the immaterial forms.

The last item in particular would tend to locate the writing in the eastern church rather than Rome. Alexandria in the second century was the chief center of Gnostic influence. Furthermore, the text contains quotations alleged to be the words of Jesus from an apocryphal Gospel of the Egyptians, of which some fragments have been preserved in citations by Clement of Alexandria. It is likely that this spurious Gospel, as its name indicates, was an Egyptian product in circulation at the time this sermon was written.[1] Finally, the fact that no early Latin manuscript has come to light, the earliest being in Greek, fits in with the internal evidence in locating it in the eastern church rather than at Rome.

But how and where did this sermon get attached to the letter known as First Clement? Was it at Corinth, to which Clement by his explicit statement addressed his letter? This is possible, for like Paul's letters and those of others it was probably circulated among the churches. A reference to the Christian life as an athletic contest in which to compete for God's laurel crown has been regarded as supporting this view, though the evidence is slender since such contests were held elsewhere as well as at Corinth and the author was doubtless familiar with Paul's use of this metaphor.

The most we can say about the circumstances of its being regarded as a second letter of Clement's is

[1] The reader may be interested in the present status of the Gospel of the Egyptians. No complete text of it has been found, or even larger fragments than were earlier available. However, we do now have the Nag Hammadi material of nearly four dozen manuscripts and some of these, notably the Gospel of Thomas, the Gospel of Philip, and the Dialogue of the Redeemer, contain sayings which closely resemble some of those quoted in Second Clement. There is no way yet of determining with certainty whether any of these came from a lost Gospel of the Egyptians or from some other source.

that some anonymous presbyter, whose name may or may not have been Clement, cared enough about the relation of the Christian faith to the issues of his time to write out his sermon, a thoughtful sermon on the things nearest his heart. Then it was added directly after the letter from the Bishop of Rome to the church at Corinth in some collection of materials for reading in the churches, and whether by accident or design it was ascribed to Clement. The fact that some parts of it are still worth reading and pondering in our day must constitute the unknown author's laurels.

1. *The New Being in Christ*

Note that the sermon is oriented as a sermon should be—it begins by centering attention on Christ and what he has done for our salvation. "When we think little of him, we also hope to receive little." The picture of those to whom it is addressed as blinded by false gods and the works of men until the mist is rolled back by a clearer vision of Christ speaks to us today, as does the author's almost Tillichian reference to the contrast between "not being" and "coming to be."

Brethren, we must think of Jesus Christ, as we do of God, as the judge of living and dead, and we must not think lightly of our salvation. For when we think little of him, we also hope to receive little. And those who listen as though to small matters

106

sin, and we sin, not knowing whence we were
called, and by whom, and to what place, and what
sufferings Jesus Christ endured for us. What re-
turn, then, can we make to him, or what fruit can
we offer worthy of his gift to us? How many blessings do we owe to him? For he has given us the
light, as a Father he has acknowledged us as sons,
he saved us when we were perishing. What praise,
then, can we give him, or what repayment for what
we have received? We were blind in mind, worshiping stone and wood and gold and silver, the
works of men, and our whole life was nothing but
death. So when we were enveloped in darkness,
with our sight so full of mist, we received our sight
back, and laid aside by his will the cloud that enveloped us. For he has taken pity on us, and merci-
fully saved us, seeing in us our great error and ruin,
and that we had no hope of salvation except from
him. For he called us when we were no more, and
from not being he willed that we should come to be.

COMPARE II COR. 4:1-6; I PET. 2:9-10.

2. *Words and Works*

As vigorously as anyone who now calls for the renewal of the church, the author insists that Christ is
best honored not by words alone, but by the doing of
his commandments in relation to one's fellowmen.
Some of the quotations in this passage are easily recognized, but the one with which it closes is from an

unknown source, possibly the apocryphal Gospel of
the Egyptians.

Since he has shown us such mercy, first that we
who are living do not sacrifice to those dead gods,
and do not worship them, but through him have
come to know the Father of truth, what is knowledge with reference to him if it is not refusing to
deny him through whom we have come to know
him? And he himself says, "Everyone that ack-
nowledges me before men I will acknowledge before the Father." This then, is our reward, if we
acknowledge him through whom we were saved.
But how shall we acknowledge him? By doing
what he says, and not disregarding his commandments, and honoring him not only with our lips,
but with our whole hearts and our whole minds.
For it says in Isaiah, "This people honors me with
their lips, yet their hearts are far away from me."

Let us therefore not only call him Lord, for that
will not save us. For he says, "It is not everyone
who says to me 'Lord! Lord!' who will be saved, but
he who acts uprightly." So then, brethren, let us
acknowledge him with our acts, by loving one another, by not committing adultery or speaking evil
of one another, or being jealous, but by being self-
controlled, merciful, kind. And we ought to be sym-
pathetic with one another and not to love money.
By these actions let us acknowledge him, and not
by their opposites. And we must not fear men more,
but God. Because of this, if you do these things,

the Lord said, "Even if you are gathered with me in my bosom, but do not do my commands, I will cast you off and say to you, Go away from me, I do not know whence you come, you doers of iniquity."

COMPARE ISA. 29:13-14; MATT. 7:21-23; JAS. 2 14-17.

3. *Two Worlds*

Here the author places in sharp contrast the present world with its temptations to immorality, avarice, and corruption and the blessedness of eternal life. Again we find a combination of authentic biblical citations with a conversation, of which no source is known, said to have taken place between Jesus and Peter. As in the preceding section, this may be from the Gospel of the Egyptians.

Therefore, brothers, ceasing to tarry in this world, let us do the will of Him who called us, and let us not be afraid to leave this world. For the Lord said, "You will be like lambs among wolves." But Peter replied by saying, "What if the wolves tear the lambs to pieces?" Jesus said to Peter, "After their death the lambs should not fear the wolves, nor should you fear those who kill you and can do nothing more to you. But fear him who, when you are dead, has power over soul and body to cast them into the flames of hell." You must realize, brothers, that our stay in this world of the flesh is slight and short, but Christ's promise is great and wonderful, and means rest in the coming Kingdom and in eternal life. What, then, must we do to get these things, except to lead a holy and upright life and to regard these things of the world as alien to us and not to desire them? For in wanting to obtain these things we fall from the right way.

The Lord says, "No servant can serve two masters." If we want to serve both God and money, it will do us no good. "For what good does it do a man to gain the whole world and forfeit his life?" This world and the world to come are two enemies. This one means adultery, corruption, avarice and deceit, while the other gives them up. We cannot, then, be friends of both. To get the one, we must give the other up. We think that it is better to hate what is here, for it is trifling, transitory, and perishable, and to value what is there—things good and imperishable. Yes, if we do the will of Christ, we shall find rest, but if not, nothing will save us from eternal punishment, if we fail to heed his commands. Furthermore, the Scripture also says in Ezekiel, "Though Noah and Jacob and Daniel should rise, they shall not save their children in captivity." If even such upright men as these cannot save their children by their uprightness, what assurance have we that we shall enter God's Kingdom if we fail to keep our baptism pure and undefiled? Or who will plead for us if we are not found to have holy and upright deeds?

COMPARE EZEK. 14:12-20; LUKE 12:4-5; 16:10-13.

4. *The Contest and the Crown*

Here the author shows his homiletical skill in the
use of two illustrations familiar to the experience of
those to whom the sermon is addressed. In the first
there is a note of special realism in the recognition
that if we cannot all receive the victor's crown, we
can at least aspire to come near to it. In the second
the comparison of the Christian with clay in the hands
of the potter is turned to place the emphasis not on
man's passivity before God, but on the need of repentance and active effort to meet the conditions of salvation.

So then, my brethren, let us contend, knowing
that the contest is close at hand, and that many
make voyages for corruptible prizes, but not all are
crowned, save those who have toiled much, and
contended well. Let us then contend that we may
all be crowned. Let us run the straight course, the
immortal contest, and let many of us sail to it, and
contend, that we may also receive the crown, and if
we cannot all receive the crown, let us at least
come near to it. We must remember that if he who
takes part in the contest for a corruptible prize be
detected in unfairness, he is flogged, taken up, and
thrown off the course. What do you think? What
shall he suffer who cheats in the contest for that
which is incorruptible? For of those who have not
kept the seal of baptism he says:—"Their worm
shall not die, and their fire shall not be quenched,
and they shall be a spectacle for all flesh."

Let us repent then while we are on the earth. For we are clay in the hand of the workman; for just as the potter, if he make a vessel, and it be bent or broken in his hand, models it afresh, but if he has come so far as to put it into the fiery oven, he can do nothing to mend it any more; so also let us, so long as we are in this world, repent with all our heart of the wicked deeds which we have done in the flesh, that we may be saved by the Lord, while we have a time for repentance. For after we have departed from this world, we can no longer make confession, or repent any more in that place. So then, brethren, if we do the will of the Father, if we keep the flesh pure, and if we observe the commandments of the Lord, we shall obtain eternal life. For the Lord says in the Gospel, "If ye did not guard that which is small, who shall give you that which is great? For I tell you that he who is faithful in that which is least, is faithful also in that which is much." He means, then, this:—keep the flesh pure, and the seal of baptism undefiled, that we may obtain eternal life.

COMPARE ISA. 66:24; LUKE 16: 10-12; I COR. 9:24-27.

5. *Wait in Hope and Single-Mindedness*

This passage is significant not only for its contemporary relevance but for two quotations said to be from "the prophetic word," or a saying of the Lord, but not identifiable in the Bible. The first of these in regard to the patience taught by the slow ripening of the grape is found also in First Clement, though without the concluding word of application. The second, which stresses purity and single-mindedness—"the outside as the inside"—is quoted by Clement of Alexandria, who states that it is from the Gospel of the Egyptians.

Let us then serve God with a pure heart, and we shall be righteous, but if we do not serve him, because we do not believe the promise of God, we shall be miserable. For the prophetic word also says:—"Miserable are the double-minded that doubt in their heart, who say, These things we heard long ago and in the time of our fathers, but we have waited from day to day, and have seen none of them. O foolish men! compare yourselves to a tree; take a vine; first it sheds its leaves, then there comes a bud, after this the unripe grape, then the full bunch. So also my people has had tumults and afflictions; afterwards it shall receive the good things." Therefore, my brethren, let us not be double-minded, but let us be patient in hope, that we may also receive the reward. For he is faithful who promised to pay to each man the recompense of his deeds. If then we do righteousness before God we shall enter into his kingdom, and shall receive the promises "which ear hath not heard, nor hath eye seen, neither hath it entered into the heart of man."

Let us then wait for the kingdom of God, from hour to hour, in love and righteousness, seeing that we know not the day of the appearing of God. For when the Lord himself was asked by someone when his kingdom would come, he said: "When the two shall be one, and the outside as the inside, and the male with the female neither male nor female." Now "the two are one" when we speak with one another in truth, and there is but one soul in two bodies without dissimulation. And by "the outside as the inside" he means this, that the inside is the soul, and the outside is the body. Therefore, just as your body is visible, so let your soul be apparent in your good works. And by "the male with the female neither male nor female" he means this, that when a brother sees a sister he should have no thought of her as female, nor she of him as male. When you do this, he says, the kingdom of my Father will come.

COMPARE MARK 4:26-29; GAL. 3:28; JAS. 1:5-8.

6. *The Living Church*

These two very different approaches have a common theme—the importance of manifesting Christ in the lives of church members. The first is a simple and straightforward statement, very relevant to the current mood today, that outsiders are alienated by the failure of those within the church to observe the love commandments of Jesus. The second is a subtle elaboration of the thought that the preexistent church, created before all else, became incarnate in the flesh of Jesus and continues in the flesh of its members through the Holy Spirit if they remain faithful and pure in their living.

And let us not try to please men, or wish to please only ourselves, but also the outsiders, by our uprightness, in order that the name may not be reproached because of us. For the Lord says, "My name is continually reproached among all the heathen," and again, "Woe to the man because of whom my name is reproached." Why is it reproached? Because you do not do what I want. For when the heathen hear from our mouths the oracles of God, they wonder at them as beautiful and great; but afterward when they find out that what we do is unworthy of the things we say, they turn from it too and revile it, declaring it a myth and a delusion. For when they hear us say that God says, "It is no merit in you if you love those who love you, but you have merit if you love your enemies and those who hate you"—when they hear that, they wonder at such extraordinary goodness; but when they see that not only do we not love those who hate us but not even those who love us, they laugh at us, and the name is reviled.

Therefore, brethren, if we do the will of God our Father, we shall belong to the first church, that spiritual one, that was created before the sun and moon; but if we do not do the will of God, we shall be of those meant by the scripture that says, "My house has become a robbers' cave." So, then, let us choose to be part of the church of life, in order that we may be saved. I do not suppose you are unaware that a living "church is the body of Christ"; for the scripture says, "God made man male and female." The male is Christ, the female is the church. Besides, the books and the apostles say that the church not only exists now, but has done so from the beginning. For she was spiritual as our Jesus also was, but he was revealed in the last days, to save us. And the church, which was spiritual, was revealed in the flesh of Christ, showing us that if any of us guards her in the flesh and does not corrupt her, he will get her back again in the holy Spirit. For this flesh is a copy of the spirit. No one therefore who has spoiled the copy will share in the original. So what he means is this, brethren: preserve the flesh, so that you may share in the spirit. But if we say that the flesh is the church and the spirit is Christ, then the man who outrages the flesh outrages the church. Such a man therefore will not share in the spirit which is Christ. Such is the life and immortality this flesh can share in, if it is joined to the holy Spirit, and no one can say or tell what the Lord has prepared for his chosen.

COMPARE LUKE 6:27-36, 46; EPH. 1:3-14.

The Letter to Diognetus

It has been noted repeatedly that it is difficult to date with precision these early post-biblical writings, though there are sufficient grounds for placing most of them between the last decade of the first century of the Christian era and the middle of the second. In what is traditionally known as the Epistle to Diognetus, the evidence becomes still more indistinct.

In the first place, it does not read much like a letter but like what might in official language be called a "white paper," or exposition of a situation.

117

The first ten chapters, which differ considerably from the last two, give an exposition and defense of the way Christians live and of the supernatural grounds of the Christian life and of the Christian revelation. Thus the writing forms a bridge between the type of literature produced by the Apostolic Fathers, whose work we have examined, and the more philosophically oriented Apologists, who succeeded them. The last two chapters, probably the work of another hand, are in the mood of a sermon and were probably intended as a homily either for Epiphany or for Easter.

The authorship is unknown as is the date of either part of the writing. One theory with considerable support holds that the first part was written by Quadratus in Asia Minor as a defense of the Christians to the Emperor Hadrian in the third decade of the second century; the second part, by Hippolytus considerably later. Other scholars would place the entire document in the latter part of the second century.

And who was Diognetus to whom the letter is addressed? Was he the Diognetus who tutored the lad of the royal court who was destined to become the Stoic philosopher-emperor Marcus Aurelius Antonius whose dates are 121-80? This is the traditional view. Or an official in Hadrian's court? Or some unknown but important person who could be addressed as "His Excellency"? We simply do not know.

Nor can we be sure that we have an accurate text, for the one early manuscript that had been preserved in the municipal library at Strasbourg until a century ago was burned during the German attack on that city on August 24, 1870. Fortunately, however, copies had been made. There is an abrupt break in the seventh chapter which indicates that something had been dropped out, but this appears to have occurred before the Strasbourg manuscript was copied from a still earlier original.

Yet none of these unsolved problems of date and authorship impair the beauty and richness of the writing. The description given by the author of the Christian within the world, in it but not surrendering to its claims, maintaining in his living a unique identity like the soul within the body, is so apt a description of the Christian ideal that it is often quoted today. It is doubtless the most familiar of all these early post-biblical writings. We shall note also the author's vivid description of the God-given character of the Christian life, of the long purposes of God as he fashions the "new race" of Christians within the historical scene, and the guiding presence of the Christ, or Logos, in all creation. That the author was strongly influenced by Paul's second letter to the Corinthians and by the Gospel of John will be noted. Yet the author was no mere copyist; he had a grasp of the Christian message and its meaning that makes his words come through to us still with vitality and power.

119

1. *How to Listen*

The author begins his message to Diognetus with counsel that might well be taken to heart today by those who listen to the gospel message in either its spoken or written form. Whether interested inquirers, skeptics, or like many of us, ones so long accustomed to hearing it that it has lost its cutting edge, all need to "pack away old ideas" and "become like new men" if the message is to be heard in its richness and power.

To His Excellency, Diognetus:

I understand, sir, that you are really interested in learning about the religion of the Christians, and that you are making an accurate and careful investigation of the subject. You want to know, for instance, what God they believe in and how they worship him, while at the same time they disregard the world and look down on death, and how it is that they do not treat the divinities of the Greeks as gods at all, although on the other hand they do not follow the superstition of the Jews. You would also like to know the source of the loving affection that they have for each other. You wonder, too, why this new race or way of life has appeared on earth now and not earlier. I certainly welcome this keen interest on your part, and I ask God, who gives us the power to speak and the power to listen, to let me speak in such a way that you may derive the greatest possible benefit from the listening, and to enable you to listen to such good effect that I may never have a reason for regretting what I have said.

Now, then, clear out all the thoughts that take up your attention, and pack away all the old ways of looking at things that keep deceiving you. You must become like a new man from the beginning, since, as you yourself admit, you are going to listen to a really new message.

COMPARE I COR. 1:18-25; 2:6-13.

2. *The Church in the World*

After some caustic words about the stupidity of the Greeks in worshiping man-made idols and the errors of the Jews in their sacrificial offerings and taboos, the author's mood shifts to a positive appraisal of the living of Christians within an alien environment. In a day when much is being said about the importance of Christian life and service in a largely secular world, this passage has unusual interest and relevance.

For Christians cannot be distinguished from the rest of the human race by country or language or customs. They do not live in cities of their own; they do not use a peculiar form of speech; they do not follow an eccentric manner of life. This doctrine of theirs has not been discovered by the ingenuity or deep thought of inquisitive men, nor do they put forward a merely human teaching, as some people do. Yet, although they live in Greek and barbarian cities alike, as each man's lot has been cast, and follow the customs of the country in cloth-

121

ing and food and other matters of daily living, at the same time they give proof of the remarkable and admittedly extraordinary constitution of their own commonwealth. They live in their own countries, but only as aliens. They have a share in everything as citizens, and endure everything as foreigners. Every foreign land is their fatherland, and yet for them every fatherland is a foreign land. They marry, like everyone else, and they beget children, but they do not cast out their offspring. They share their board with each other, but not their marriage bed. It is true that they are "in the flesh," but they do not live "according to the flesh." They busy themselves on earth, but their citizenship is in heaven. They obey the established laws, but in their own lives they go far beyond what the laws require. They love all men, and by all men are persecuted. They are unknown, and still they are condemned; they are put to death, and yet they are brought to life. They are poor, and yet they make many rich; they are completely destitute, and yet they enjoy complete abundance. They are dishonored, and in their very dishonor are glorified; they are defamed, and are vindicated. They are reviled, and yet they bless; when they are affronted, they still pay due respect. When they do good, they are punished as evildoers; undergoing punishment, they rejoice because they are brought to life. They are treated by the Jews as foreigners and enemies, and are hunted down by the Greeks; and all the time those who hate them find it impossible to justify their enmity.

To put it simply: What the soul is in the body, that Christians are in the world. The soul is dispersed through all the members of the body, and Christians are scattered through all the cities of the world. The soul dwells in the body but does not belong to the body, and Christians dwell in the world, but do not belong to the world. The soul, which is invisible, is kept under guard in the visible body; in the same way, Christians are recognized when they are in the world, but their religion remains unseen. The flesh hates the soul and treats it as an enemy, even though it has suffered no wrong, because it is prevented from enjoying its pleasures; so too the world hates Christians, even though it suffers no wrong at their hands, because they range themselves against its pleasures. The soul loves the flesh that hates it, and its members; in the same way, Christians love those who hate them. The soul is shut up in the body, and yet itself holds the body together; while Christians are restrained in the world as in a prison, and yet themselves hold the world together. The soul, which is immortal, is housed in a mortal dwelling; while Christians are settled among corruptible things, to wait for the incorruptibility that will be theirs in heaven. The soul, when faring badly as to food and drink, grows better; so too Christians, when punished, day by day increase more and more. It is to

123

no less a post than this that God has ordered them, and they must not try to evade it.

COMPARE II COR. 6:1-10; EPH. 2:19-22; PHIL. 3:20.

3. *All Things Were Made Through Him*

In a passage of unusual eloquence and beauty, the writer presents Christ as God's agent in the creation of the entire universe and also as God and King, who is sent as man to men to rule the world, not with tyranny and compulsion, but by gentleness and persuasion. The author doubtless owes his concept of the creation of the world by the preexistent Christ to the prologue of John's Gospel and similar statements in Colossians and Hebrews, but he elaborates it to a greater degree than do any of the biblical writers.

As I have indicated, it is not an earthly discovery that was committed to them; it is not a mortal thought that they think of as worth guarding with such care, nor have they been entrusted with the stewardship of merely human mysteries. On the contrary, it was really the Ruler of all, the Creator of all, the invisible God himself, who from heaven established the truth and the holy, incomprehensible word among men, and fixed it firmly in their hearts. Nor, as one might suppose, did he do this by sending to men some subordinate—an angel, or principality, or one of those who administer earthly affairs, or perhaps one of those to whom the govern-

ment of things in heaven is entrusted. Rather, he
sent the Designer and Maker of the universe himself, by whom he created the heavens and confined
the sea within its own bounds—him whose hidden
purposes all the elements of the world faithfully
carry out, him from whom the sun has received the
measure of the daily rounds that it must keep, him
whom the moon obeys when he commands her to
shine by night, and whom the stars obey as they
follow the course of the moon. He sent him by
whom all things have been set in order and distinguished and placed in subjection—the heavens
and the things that are in the heavens, the earth
and the things in the earth, the sea and the things
in the sea, fire, air, the unfathomed pit, the things
in the heights and in the depths and in the realm
between; God sent him to men.

Now, did he send him, as a human mind might
assume, to rule by tyranny, fear, and terror? Far
from it! He sent him out of kindness and gentleness, like a king sending his son who is himself a
king. He sent him as God; he sent him as man to
men. He willed to save man by persuasion, not by
compulsion, for compulsion is not God's way of
working. In sending him, God called men, but did
not pursue them; he sent him in love, not in judgment. Yet he will indeed send him someday as our
Judge, and who shall stand when he appears?

COMPARE JOHN 1:1-5; COL. 1:15-20; HEB. 1:1-4.

4. *The Imitation of God*

The imitation of Christ is a familiar term, made so by the title of an immortal classic of the Christian life probably written by Gerhard Groote, though it bears the name of its editor and copyist Thomas à Kempis. Occasionally one is told that the term is blasphemous, since no man can imitate the Son of God. But what of imitating God himself? Our author does not hesitate to say that this is possible—he tells how to do it! Leaving both blasphemy and eschatology aside, there is sound Christian wisdom in his counsel.

If you too yearn for this faith, then first of all you must acquire full knowledge of the Father. For God loved men, and made the world for their sake, and put everything on earth under them. He gave them reason and intelligence, and to them alone he entrusted the capacity for looking upward to him, since he formed them after his own image. It was to them that he sent his only-begotten Son, and to them he promised the Kingdom in heaven which he will give to those who love him. And when you have acquired this knowledge, think with what joy you will be filled! Think how you will love him, who first loved you so! And when you love him, you will be an imitator of his goodness. And do not be surprised to learn that a man can become an imitator of God. He can, because God wills it.

To be happy does not, indeed, consist in lording over one's neighbors, or in longing to have some advantage over the weaker ones, or in being rich and ordering one's inferiors about. It is not in this way that any man can imitate God, for such things are alien to his majesty. But if a man takes his neighbor's burden on himself, and is willing to help his inferior in some respect in which he himself is better off, and, by providing the needy with what he himself possesses because he has received it from God, becomes a god to those who receive it—then this man is an imitator of God. Then, while your lot is cast on earth, you will realize that God rules in heaven; then you will begin to talk of the mysteries of God; then you will love and admire those who are being punished for their refusal to deny God; then you will condemn the fraud and error of the world, once you really understand the true life in heaven, once you look down on the apparent death here below, once you fear the real death kept for those who are condemned to the eternal fire, which will punish to the end those that are handed over to it. Then you will admire those who for righteousness' sake endure the transitory fire, and will call them happy, when you learn about that other fire.

COMPARE GEN. 1:26-28; JAS. 1:16-27.

5. *The Eternal and Present Word*

This is a moving tribute to the Word made flesh to become the living Christ, the Logos who was from the beginning yet is "ever born young in the hearts of the saints." To the author here is the true source of

127

the grace and greatness of the church. And should it not be so with us?

This is he who was from the beginning, who appeared new and was found to be old, and is ever born young in the hearts of the saints. This is the eternal one, who today is accounted a Son, by whom the Church is made rich and grace is multiplied as it unfolds among the saints—the grace that gives understanding, makes mysteries plain, announces seasons, rejoices in believers, is given freely to seekers, that is, to such as do not break the pledges of their faith, or go beyond the bounds set by the fathers. Then the reverence taught by the Law is hymned, and the grace given to the Prophets is recognized, and the faith of the Gospels is made secure, and the tradition of the apostles is maintained, and the grace of the Church exults. And if you do not grieve this grace, you will understand what the Logos speaks, through whom he pleases and whenever he chooses. For we simply share with you, out of love for the things that have been revealed to us, everything that we have been prompted to speak out under stress, in obedience to the will and commandment of the Logos.

COMPARE JOHN 1:14-18; PHIL. 4:4-9.

6. *The Tree of Knowledge and the Tree of Life*

This is a very meaningful passage in which the author uses the symbolism of Gen. 2:8-9 and 3:1-7 to compare the church to the original paradise and to point out, as many contemporary interpretations of the fall of man fail to do, that the tree of knowledge is also God's good gift and as essential to the Christian as is the tree of life. Together, and only when they are possessed together, is true Christian fruit-bearing possible.

If you read this, and listen to it earnestly, you will discover what God has prepared for those who love him as they ought, and have become a Paradise of delight, cultivating in themselves a flourishing tree, rich with all kinds of fruit, while they themselves are decked out with a variety of fruits; for in this Garden a tree of knowledge and a tree of life have been planted. But it is not the tree of knowledge that destroys; it is disobedience that brings destruction. Indeed, there is a deep meaning in the passage of Scripture which tells how God in the beginning planted a tree of knowledge and a tree of life in the midst of Paradise, to show that life is attained through knowledge. It was because the first men did not use this knowledge with clean hearts that they were stripped of it by the deceit of the serpent. For there cannot be life without knowledge any more than there can be sound knowledge without genuine life, and so the two trees were planted close together. Because the apostle saw the force of this, he found fault with the knowledge that is put into effect in life without regard to the reality of the commandment, pointing out that "knowledge puffs up, but love builds up." For the man who thinks he knows anything apart from knowledge that is genuine and borne out by life has actually learned nothing, but is deceived by the serpent, because he does not love life. But he who has gained full knowledge with reverence and seeks after life can plant in hope and look for fruit.

COMPARE GEN. 2:8-9; I COR. 8:1-3; COL. 1: 9-14.

The Odes of Solomon

We now bring to a close this compilation from
the writings of the group usually referred to as the
Apostolic Fathers. We have seen that their writings
mainly, though not wholly, are to be dated from
the first half of the second century, and although
they contain some turgid passages, they reflect the
"first fine careless rapture" of Christian faith. Just
beyond them in the latter part of the century are
the so-called Apologists, of whom the ablest and
most influential was Justin the Martyr with Aris-
tides, Tatian, Athenagoras, and Theophilus as subordinate figures. All these tend to give to Chris-

tianity a philosophical slant in an effort to make it congenial to Greek thought and to show its superiority to pagan faiths. These writings are important from the standpoint of church history and the history of Christian thought but contain little that could be termed devotional writing.

However, within the first half of the second century another type of Christian writing appeared. This is known to scholars, but too little attention is paid to it, and it is perhaps a safe guess that most Christian ministers and laymen have never heard of it. This is the poetry found in the first Christian hymnbook.

Here amid some awkward passages (is any hymnbook free from them?) are found some poems of great beauty, reflecting deep spiritual experience and radiant with Christian joy. The form is marked by the parallelism characteristic of Hebrew poetry, but the content is Christian. There are forty-two of these poems, for the most part hymns of praise and Christian witness which express the gratitude of the believer for what God in Christ has done for him in the remaking of his life.

This hymnbook is known as the Odes of Solomon, though the name of Solomon is wholly pseudonymous. It may have been so called to give it the aura of wisdom in line with the apocryphal pre-Christian book entitled the Wisdom of Solomon. Yet the title may have a more authentic justification in the implication that Christ, not Solomon, is the true exemplar of wisdom.

The discovery of this first Christian hymnbook is relatively recent. It was known to scholars that such a collection of poems, or psalms, had once existed, for there are traces of them in other early Syriac literature, in the Gnostic *Pistis Sophia,* in the writings of Eusebius and in the works of the Roman scholar Lactantius in the fourth century. A text of the Psalms of Solomon, written in Hebrew with a Jewish flavor, had survived, and it was thought that the Odes might be part of the same compilation. However, in 1909 the British scholar J. Rendel Harris discovered near the Tigris River in Mesopotamia a nearly complete text of the Odes of Solomon. It is written in Syriac, which is a dialect of Aramaic, akin to but not identical with the Aramaic spoken by Jesus. A partial text in Coptic is also available. Although the name of Jesus does not appear in the manuscript, its frequent references to the Son, to the Holy Spirit, and to the Word as having come in human form for man's salvation make it clear that it is a book of Christian poetry.

There is little doubt that this work is authentic, though questions remain. What is its relation to the Gospel of John? Is the Logos doctrine of the Odes based upon its prologue, or do both have a common source? Was it written originally in Greek or Syriac? No Greek text has been found, though it was probably quoted from in Greek or Latin. Opinions among scholars differ. If it was originally written in Greek, they tend to locate the writing at

Antioch at or near the time of Ignatius; if in Syriac, at Edessa in northwestern Mesopotamia.

We cannot settle the question, but there is considerable evidence in favor of a Syriac original. At Edessa there was a strong Christian church which produced some important Christian literature. Edessa was the center of Syriac-speaking Christianity. About A.D. 300 this church, which still exists as the Apostolic Armenian, became the first national church before Constantine. But our concern is earlier.

Furthermore, Edessa was not very far from Antioch, where Ignatius was bishop in the early years of the second century. There is a tradition that he encouraged the practice of singing in the services of worship, and at a number of points there are close parallels between statements of his and passages found in the Odes. This is true also of the Odes and the Letter of Barnabas. But again we do not know which was written first, and the conjunction might be coincidence though some connection seems more probable.

Where, then, do we come out? The best guess appears to be that some unknown Christian poet, possibly a contemporary of Ignatius around the turn of the century and not later than 150, composed these rhythmic verses to the glory of God. These hymns of praise were then sung in the Edessa church and probably in neighboring churches, though there is no evidence that they came into general use. Some of them may have been used in baptismal services, and a reference by Cyril of Jerusalem in the fourth century seems to so indicate. Yet, on the whole, their mood is not liturgical but deeply personal. Resurrected from a long sleep, they can now stir our hearts to worship and praise the same Redeemer.

1. *The Crown of Life*

The symbolism of the victor's crown by which Christian fidelity is honored is a frequent theme in the Odes, as it is in the New Testament. There is a difference, however, in that the New Testament writers project it into the future, while the odist puts it in the present tense. But are not both notes basic to the Christian faith? The enduring, fruit-bearing nature of the crown is reminiscent both of the "unfading crown of glory" promised in I Pet. 5:4 and of the tree of righteousness in the first psalm.

> The Lord is upon my head like a crown;
> And I shall not be without Him.
>
> The crown of truth was woven for me;
> And it caused thy branches to bud in me;
>
> For it is not like a withered crown that buddeth not:
>
> But thou livest upon my head;
> And thou hast blossomed upon my head:

135

Thy fruits are full-grown and perfect;
They are full of thy salvation.
                                        Hallelujah.[1]

COMPARE II TIM. 4:7-8; JAS. 1:12; I PET. 5:4;
REV. 2:10.

2. *A Hymn to the Love of God*

Some have objected to the mood of this ode as being
too amorous. Some of its diction suggests the Song of
Solomon in the Old Testament. However, it is essentially a Christian hymn based on the theme of I John
4:19: "We love, because he first loved us." It is no
more erotic than Charles Wesley's "Jesus, Lover of My
Soul," and this has stood the test of time!

. . . I should not have known how to love the
    Lord,
If He had not loved me.

For who is able to discern love,
Except one that is loved?

I love the Beloved, and my soul loves Him.
And where His rest is, there also am I.

And I shall be no stranger;
For with the Lord Most High and Merciful,
    there is no grudging.

[1] Words not found in the text but introduced by the
translator for completeness have been placed in parentheses
in the translations from which these excerpts are taken. I
have omitted the parentheses, since they interrupt the
free flow of the poetry in all the odes.

I have been united to Him, because the lover
has found the Beloved:
In order that I may love Him that is the Son,
I shall become a son.

For he who is united to Him who never dies,
He also will be immortal.

And he that hath pleasure in the Living One,[2]
Will become living.

This is the Spirit of the Lord, which doth not
lie,
Which teacheth the sons of men to know His
ways.

Be wise and understanding and vigilant.
Hallelujah.

COMPARE I JOHN 4:16-19; JOHN 14:1-3, 18-20.

3. *Living Water for All to Drink*

This ode opens on the poetic note of music played
in the human spirit by the Spirit of the Lord, but it
quickly shifts to the irresistible power of the Almighty.
A transitional statement that "the Lord has multiplied
His knowledge" leads into the main theme of the ode,
the spread of living water to the whole earth with its
gracious blessings for all who drink of it. The brief

[2] The reference to Christ as the Living One is often
found in the literature of the Syrian church.

reference to the temple suggests the universal, life-giving gospel of Christ. The entire poem is in the mood of an oratorio.

As the hand moves over the harp, and the strings speak;

So speaks in my members the Spirit of the Lord,
And I speak by His love.

For He destroys what is foreign,
And everything is of the Lord.

For thus He was from the beginning,
And shall be to the end.

That nothing should be His adversary,
And nothing should stand up against Him.

The Lord has multiplied His knowledge;
And was zealous that those things should be known which by His grace have been given to us.

And the praise of His name He gave us:
Our spirits praise His holy Spirit.

For there went forth a stream,
And became a river great and broad:
It swept away everything, and broke up and carried away the Temple.

And the restraints made by men were not able to restrain it,
Nor the arts of those whose business it is to restrain water.

For it spread over the face of the whole earth,
And it filled everything.

All the thirsty upon earth were given to drink
   of it:
And thirst was done away and quenched:

For from the Most High the draught was given.

Blessed then are the ministers of that draught,
Who have been entrusted with that water of His:

They have assuaged the dry lips,
And the will that had fainted they have raised
   up:

And souls that were near departing
They have held back from death:

And limbs that had fallen
They have straightened and set up:

They gave strength to their coming
And light to their eyes.

For everyone knew them in the Lord,
And they lived by the water an eternal life.
                    Hallelujah.

COMPARE PSALM 46; HAB. 2:14.

4. *A Good Captivity for Freedom*

We have here an example of a form which appears
frequently in the Odes. The author begins by speaking

as himself, then shifts to what is presented as if spoken by Christ. The thought of the captivity which is freedom echoes Paul's thought of the Christian as the slave of Christ. The reference in the words attributed to Christ as being "unpolluted" by love of the Gentiles is subtle but significant. It reflects a time when it had not yet been fully accepted that the gospel was equally for the Gentiles, and thus is a delicate slap at prejudice.

> The Lord hath directed my mouth by His Word;
>
> And He hath opened my heart by His Light.
>
> And He hath caused to dwell in me His deathless life;
>
> And gave me to speak the fruit of His peace:
>
> To convert the souls of those who are willing to come to Him;
>
> And to lead captive a good captivity for freedom.

(Christ speaks.)

> I was strengthened and made mighty and took the world captive;
>
> And the captivity became to me for the praise of the Most High and of God my Father.
>
> And the Gentiles were gathered together who had been scattered abroad:
>
> And I was unpolluted by my love for them,
> Because they confessed me in high places.

And the traces of the light were set upon
  their hearts;
And they walked in my life and were saved,
And they became my people for ever and ever.
  Hallelujah.

COMPARE GAL. 4:1-17; 5:1, 13-15.

5. *Words and the Word*

In this sublime hymn the author starts from his own
experience when his heart and his lips were filled with
the words of God. Then the poem modulates into an
affirmation of the universal Word, or Logos, which
interpenetrates all things and gives speech even to the
silent worlds. It comes to a climax in the declaration
that this Word, which is both truth and love, finds its
dwelling place in man.

He hath filled me with words of truth,
That I may proclaim Him.

And like the flow of waters, flows truth from
  my mouth,
And my lips showed forth its fruits.

And His knowledge He has caused to abound
  in me,
Because the mouth of the Lord is the true
  Word,
And the door of His light;

And the Most High hath given Him to His
worlds.

They are the interpreters of His beauty,
And the reciters of His praise,
And the confessors of His thought,
And the heralds of His mind,
And the instructors of His works.

For the swiftness of the Word is inexpressible:
And like its utterance, so is its swiftness and
sharpness:
And its course has no limit.

Never doth the Word fall, but ever standeth;
His descent and His way are incomprehensible.

For as His work is, so is His limit;
For He is the light and the dawn of thought.

And by Him the worlds spoke one to another;
And those that were silent acquired speech.

And from Him came love and concord;
And they spake one to another of what they
had.

And they were stimulated by the Word,
And they knew Him that made them,
Because they came into concord.

For the mouth of the Most High spake to
them;
And the interpretation of Himself had its
course by Him.

For the dwelling-place of the Word is man,
And His truth is love.

Blessed are they who by it have comprehended
everything,
And have known the Lord by His truth.
Hallelujah.

COMPARE PSALM 19; JOHN 1:1-18.

6. *A Psalm of Praise and Petition*

This prayer is very much in the mood of the Old
Testament psalms, though it is not a replica of any
of them. Doubtless the author in pouring out his soul
before the Lord was influenced by his familiarity with
them. Although these words could be uttered by a devout Jew as well as a Christian, note the striking figure
of speech in "the harp of thy Holy Spirit."

As the eyes of a son to his father,
So are my eyes at all times towards thee, O Lord.

For with thee are my consolations and my de-
lights.

Turn not away thy mercy from me, O Lord:
And take not thy pleasure from me.

Stretch out to me, my Lord, at all times, thy
right hand:
And be my guide even to the end, according
to thy good will.

Let me be well-pleasing before thee, because of
thy glory:

143

And because of thy name let me be saved from the Evil One.

And let thy gentleness, O Lord, abide with me, And the fruits of thy love.

Teach me the songs of thy truth That I may bring forth fruit in thee.

And the harp of thy Holy Spirit, open to me That with all its notes I may praise thee, O Lord.

And according to the multitudes of thy mercies So shalt thou give to me: And hasten to grant our petitions.

And thou art sufficient for all our needs.
Hallelujah.

COMPARE PSALM 30; 145.

7. *The Glory of the Lord and His Beauty*

Introducing this hymn with a reference to the works of man and his own calling to sing the praises of God, the author rises to a great crescendo in extolling the works of God in creation. The heavens declare the glory and the beauty of the Lord, and the worlds were made by his Word.

As the work of the husbandman is the plough-share;
And the work of the steersman is the guidance of the ship;

144

So also my work is the Psalm of the Lord in
  His praises;

My craft and my occupation are in His praises;
Because His love hath nourished my heart,
And even to my lips His fruits He poured out.

For my love is the Lord
And therefore I will sing unto Him.

For I am made strong in His praise,
And I have faith in Him.

I will open my mouth,
And His spirit will utter in me
The glory of the Lord and His beauty;

The work of His hands
And the fabric of His fingers;

For the multitude of His mercies,
And the strength of His Word.

For the Word of the Lord searches out the unseen thing,
And scrutinizes His thought.

For the eye sees His works,
And the ear hears His thought.

It is He who spread out the earth,
And settled the waters in the sea:

He expanded he heavens,
And fixed the stars;

And He fixed the creation and set it up:
And He rested from His works.

And created things run in their courses,
And work their works:
And they know not how to stand still and be idle.

And the hosts are subject to His Word.

The treasury of the light is the sun,
And the treasury of the darkness is the night.

And He made the sun for the day that it might
be bright;
But night brings darkness over the face of the
earth:

And by their reception one from the other
They speak the beauty of God.

And there is nothing that is without the Lord;
For He was before anything came into being.

And the Worlds were made by His Word,
And by the thought of His heart.

(Doxology)
Glory and honour to His name.
Hallelujah.

COMPARE GENESIS 1; PSALM 8; HEB. 11:1-3.

8. *A Priest of the Lord*

This poem is somewhat more subtle than it appears
on the surface. The author announces that he is a

priest of the Lord and then gives his credentials. He
has nothing to say about any sacerdotal authority. All
that he seems to be concerned about is "the offering
of His thought," righteousness, moral purity, concern
for neighbor, and the grace and glory of the Lord.

> I am a priest of the Lord;
> And to Him I do priestly service;
>
> And to Him I offer the offering of His
> thought.
>
> For His thought is not like the thought of the
> world,
> Nor like the thought of the flesh;
> Nor like them that serve carnally.
>
> The offering of the Lord is righteousness;
> And purity of heart and lips.
>
> Offer your reins before Him blamelessly;
> And let not thy heart do violence to heart;
> Nor thy soul do violence to soul.
>
> Thou shalt not acquire a stranger by the
> blood of thy soul; [3]
> Neither shalt thou seek to deal guilefully
> with thy neighbour;
> Neither shalt thou deprive him of the cover-
> ing of his nakedness.

[3] The translator omits "by the blood of thy soul," saying that it is in the text but does not make sense. It seems
to me that it does. It is a bold but arresting figure.

But put on the grace of the Lord without stint;
And come into His Paradise and make thee
a garland from His tree;

And put it on thy head and be glad;
And recline on His rest;

And His glory shall go before thee;
And thou shalt receive of His kindness and
His grace:
And thou shalt be fat in truth in the praise
of His holiness.

(Doxology)

Praise and honour to His name.
Hallelujah.

COMPARE ISA. 58:1-12.

9. *Who Can Write the Songs of the Lord?*

In this lovely psalm both the confidence and the humility of the writer are evident. His heart overflows in praise to the Lord; the whole earth gives witness to God's goodness and greatness. Yet the challenge to try to interpret the wonders of the Lord overwhelms him. So "it suffices to know and to rest," while the river of divine grace flows on to the help of those in need. Have not many of us shared his mood?

I poured out praise to the Lord;
For I am His:

And I will speak His holy song,
For my heart is with Him.

For His harp is in my hands,
And the songs of His rest shall not be silent.

I will cry unto Him with my whole heart;
I will praise and exalt Him with all my
members.

For from the East and even to the West
Praise is His:

And from the South even to the North
Confession is His:

And from the top of the hills to their utmost
bound
Perfection is His.

Who can write the songs of the Lord,
Or who read them:

Or who can train his soul for life,
That his soul may be saved?

Or who can rest on the Most High,
That from His mouth he may speak?

O that one were able to interpret the wonders
of the Lord!
For though he who could interpret were to
be dissolved,
Yet that which is interpreted would remain.

For it suffices to know and to rest;
For in the rest the singers stand;

> Like a river which has an abundant source,
> And flows to the help of them that seek it.
> Hallelujah.

COMPARE Ps. 33:1-9; II Cor. 9:15.

10. *The Lord Is My Hope*

This poem clearly reflects the influence of the Old Testament Psalter, and except for the author's explicit statement that he has believed in the Lord's Messiah and seen that he was the Lord, this might not appear to be a Christian hymn. It is a good example of an apt Christian use of the Old Testament heritage. It is not quite clear whether "to make war by His Word and to take victory by His power" is simply an Old Testament echo, but since the early Christians did not engage in military conflict, we may assume that it refers to spiritual warfare.

> The Lord is my hope:
> In Him I shall not be confounded.
>
> And according to His praise He made me,
> And according to His goodness even so He gave unto me.
>
> And according to His mercies He exalted me;
> And according to His excellent beauty He set me on high.
>
> And He brought me up out of the depths of Sheol;
> And from the mouth of death He drew me.

And I laid my enemies low;
And He justified me by His grace.

For I believed in the Lord's Messiah
And I saw that He was the Lord.

And He showed me His sign,
And led me by His light.

And He gave me the staff of His power;
That I might subdue the imaginations of the
    people,
And bring down the power of the men of might:

To make war by His Word,
And to take victory by His power.

And the Lord overthrew my enemy by His Word;
And he became like the stubble which the wind
    carries away.
And I gave praise to the Most High;
Because He exalted His servant and the son of
    His handmaid.

Hallelujah.

COMPARE Ps. 31:1-5; 33:10-22.

11. *Water from the Living Fountain*

The imagery in this hymn is found elsewhere in the
Odes as well as in the Bible. Yet the poem is such a
beautiful tribute in praise of the living water promised to the thirsty that any lack of originality may well

be overlooked. The translator's note indicates that "fill ye water" instead of the more prosaic "draw water" is a decidedly Aramaic touch.

> Fill ye water for yourselves from the living
>   fountain of the Lord:
> For it has been opened to you:
>
> And come all ye thirsty and take a draught;
> And rest by the fountain of the Lord.
>
> For fair it is and pure;
> And it gives rest to the soul.
>
> Much sweeter is its water than honey;
> And the honeycomb of bees is not to be com-
>   pared with it.
>
> For it flows from the lips of the Lord,
> And from the heart of the Lord is its name.
>
> And it came unlimited and invisible;
> And until it was set in the midst they did
>   not know it.
>
> Blessed are they who have drunk therefrom;
> And rested thereby.
>   Hallelujah.

COMPARE JOHN 4:7-15; REV. 22:1-5.

12. *Believe and Live*

This simple but sturdy little poem is unlike any other in the entire collection. It has no specific scriptural basis, but appears to be a picture of "the peace of God, which passes all understanding." Since the final couplet marks it as Christian, we are not to understand the one before it as denying the existence of the world around us, but its self-sufficiency.

> There is no hard way where there is a simple heart;
> Nor is there any barrier where the thoughts are upright;
> Nor is there any storm in the depth of the illuminated thought.
>
> The one who is surrounded on every side by open country
> Is freed from doubts.
>
> The likeness of that which is below
> Is that which is above;
>
> For everything is above;
> And below there is nothing, but it is believed to be by the ignorant.
>
> Grace has been revealed for your salvation:
> Believe and live and be saved.
> Hallelujah.

COMPARE PHIL. 4:4-13.

13. *The Dew of the Lord*

This hymn is very much in the mood of Whittier's "Drop Thy still dews of quietness," although it is

doubtful that Whittier ever heard of the Odes of Solomon. And does not the reference to a prevailing state
of fear with "a smoke and a judgment" as the result
describe our day? The figure of being carried like a
child in the arms of its mother and being nourished
with "milk, the dew of the Lord" is a bold one, but
very suggestive.

The dew of the Lord overshadowed me in quietness,
And a cloud of peace it caused to rise over my
head;

That it might guard me continually;
And it became salvation to me:

Everybody was shaken and affrighted;
And there came from them a smoke and a judgment:

But I was keeping quiet in the ranks of the
Lord;
More than shadow was He to me, and more
than support:

And I was carried like a child by its mother;
And He gave me milk, the dew of the Lord.

And I grew great by His bounty:
And I rested in His perfection:

And I spread out my hands in the lifting up of
my soul;

And I directed myself towards the Most High,
And I was redeemed before Him:
> Hallelujah.

COMPARE MARK 10:13-16; JOHN 14:27; 16:31-33.

14. *Hallelujah!*

The title chosen for this last excerpt to be quoted
could apply equally to any of the others, for in all of
them is the sound of triumphant, grateful praise. Yet
there may be a special appropriateness in the fact that
here the author in his glad exultation brings together
so many figures of speech that they build one upon
another to constitute a richly blended chorus of adoration and Christian confidence.

As the honey distils from the comb of the bees,
And the milk flows from the woman that loves
her children,
So also is my hope on thee, my God.

As the fountain gushes out its water,
So my heart gushes out the praise of the Lord,
And my lips utter praises to Him.

And my tongue is sweet in His intimate con-
verse
And my limbs are made fat by the sweetness
of His odes.

155

And my face is glad with His exultation;
And my spirit exults in His love;
And my soul shines in Him;

And the fearful one shall confide in Him;
And redemption shall in Him stand assured;

And his gain is immortal life;
And those who participate in it are incorruptible.

Hallelujah.

COMPARE PSALM 145.

References

Bibliographical data for the books from which translations have been used appear with the first excerpt from each and subsequently are indicated by the name of the translator and the page reference. Unless otherwise stated, the form used by the translator, including spelling and punctuation, has been retained.

Numerals refer to chapters in the original documents unless preceded by a colon, in which case they indicate subsections. For greater smoothness in reading, the text has been presented without subsection numbers.

First Clement

1. The First Letter of Clement to the Corinthians, 1, 2. From *The Apostolic Fathers*, English translation by Kirsopp Lake, I, 9-13.

2. *Ibid.*, 19, 20. Lake, I, 43-45.
3. *Ibid.*, 37–38. From *The Apostolic Fathers: An American Translation* by Edgar J. Goodspeed, pp. 67-68.
4. *Ibid.*, 49, 50. Lake, I, 93-97.
5. *Ibid.*, 59–61. Lake, I, 111-17.
6. *Ibid.*, 64–65. Lake, 1, 119-21.

Ignatius

1. The Letters of Ignatius. Ephesians, Intro., 3, 9, 14. Lake, I, 173, 177, 189.
2. Ephesians, 15. From *Early Christian Fathers*, Library of Christian Classics, Vol. I, translated by Cyril C. Richardson, p. 92.
3. Ephesians, 10, 13. Goodspeed, pp. 210, 211.
4. Ephesians, 4; Polycarp, Intro., 1–2. Lake, I, 177-79, 267-71.
5. Ephesians, 20; Philadelphians, 4; Polycarp, 6:2. Lake, I, 195, 243, 275.
6. Trallians, 9–11. Richardson, pp. 100-101.
7. Philadelphians, 8:2–9:2. Richardson, pp. 110-11.
8. Trallians, 12–13. Goodspeed, p. 220.

Polycarp

1. The Letter to the Philippians, 8–10. Goodspeed, pp. 242-43.
2. *Ibid.*, 11. Goodspeed, p. 243.
3. The Martyrdom of Polycarp, 8–15:1*a*, 18. From *Early Christian Fathers*, Library of Christian Classics, Vol. I, translated by Massey Hamilton Shepherd, Jr., pp. 151-54, 156.

The Shepherd of Hermas

1. The Shepherd of Hermas, Vision III, 5–6. Goodspeed, pp. 112-14.

2. *Ibid.*, 8:1-8. Goodspeed, pp. 114-15.
3. Mandate V, 2. Lake, II, 91-95.
4. Mandate VIII, 1:8-12. Lake, II, 105-7.
5. Similitude IX, 32–33. Lake, II, 295-97.

The Letter of Barnabas

1. The Letter of Barnabas, 1. Lake, I, 341-43.
2. *Ibid.*, 2. Lake, I, 343-47. (Paragraphing mine.)
3. *Ibid.*, 3. Goodspeed, p. 25.
4. *Ibid.*, 10:1-5, 9-10. Goodspeed, pp. 33-35.
5. *Ibid.*, 16:6-10. Lake, I, 397-99.

The Didache

1. The Didache, or The Teaching of the Twelve Apostles, 1–4. Goodspeed, pp. 11-14.
2. *Ibid.*, 5–6:2. Goodspeed, p. 14.
3. *Ibid.*, 9, 10. Goodspeed, pp. 15-16.
4. *Ibid.*, 14–15. Richardson, p. 178.

Second Clement

1. The So-called Second Letter of Clement, 1. Goodspeed, p. 85.
2. *Ibid.*, 3–4. Goodspeed, pp. 86-87.
3. *Ibid.*, 5–6. Richardson, p. 195.
4. *Ibid.*, 7–8. Lake, I, 139-41.
5. *Ibid.*, 11–12. Lake, I, 145-49.
6. *Ibid.*, 13:1b–14:4. Goodspeed, pp. 90-92.

The Letter to Diognetus

1. The Letter to Diognetus, 1–2:1a. From *Early Christian Fathers*, Library of Christian Classics, Vol. I, translated by Eugene R. Fairweather, pp. 213-14.

2. *Ibid.*, 5–6. Fairweather, pp. 216-18.
3. *Ibid.*, 7:1-6. Fairweather, pp. 218-19.
4. *Ibid.*, 10. Fairweather, pp. 221-22.
5. *Ibid.*, 11:4-8. Fairweather, pp. 222-23.
6. *Ibid.*, 12:1-6. Fairweather, pp. 223-24.

The Odes of Solomon

1. Ode I. From *The Odes and Psalms of Solomon,* Vol. II, edited and translated by Rendel Harris and Alphonse Mingana, p. 207. Published for the John Rylands Library at the University Press, Manchester, and by Longmans, Green & Co., London and New York, 1920. Used by permission of the John Rylands Library.
2. Ode III, Vss. 3-11. From *The Oldest Christian Hymn-Book* by Michael MarYosip, p. 40. Adapted from the Harris-Mingana edition with changes and published by Gresham's, Temple, Texas, in 1948. Used by permission of Gresham's and Mrs. Michael MarYosip.
3. Ode VI. Harris-Mingana, pp. 232-33.
4. Ode X. Harris-Mingana, pp. 263-64.
5. Ode XII. MarYosip, pp. 55-56.
6. Ode XIV. MarYosip, pp. 56-57.
7. Ode XVI. Harris-Mingana, pp. 282-84.
8. Ode XX. Harris-Mingana, pp. 312-13.
9. Ode XXVI. MarYosip, pp. 73-74.
10. Ode XXIX. MarYosip, pp. 76-77.
11. Ode XXX. Harris-Mingana, p. 366.
12. Ode XXXIV. Harris-Mingana, p. 378.
13. Ode XXXV. MarYosip, pp. 82-83.
14. Ode XL. Harris-Mingana, pp. 397-98.